ALSO BY NATHAN THRALL

The Only Language They Understand:
Forcing Compromise in Israel and Palestine

A DAY IN THE LIFE
OF ABED SALAMA

A DAY
IN THE LIFE
OF ABED
SALAMA

Anatomy of a
Jerusalem Tragedy

NATHAN THRALL

Metropolitan Books
Henry Holt and Company   New York

Metropolitan Books
Henry Holt and Company
Publishers since 1866
120 Broadway
New York, New York 10271
www.henryholt.com

Metropolitan Books® and ▥® are registered trademarks of
Macmillan Publishing Group, LLC.

Distributed in Canada by Raincoast Book Distribution Limited

Library of Congress Cataloging-in-Publication Data

Names: Thrall, Nathan, author.
Title: A day in the life of Abed Salama : anatomy of a Jerusalem tragedy /
  Nathan Thrall.
Description: First edition. | New York: Metropolitan Books, Henry Holt and
  Company, 2023. | Includes bibliographical references and index.
Identifiers: LCCN 2023017070 (print) | LCCN 2023017071 (ebook) |
  ISBN 9781250854971 (hardcover) | ISBN 9781250854988 (ebook)
Subjects: LCSH: Jewish-Arab relations. | Palestinian Arabs—Israel—Social
  conditions. | Salama, Abed. | Parental grief—Israel. | Arab-Israeli conflict—
  1993– | Jerusalem—Social conditions.
Classification: LCC DS119.76 .T488 2023 (print) | LCC DS119.76 (ebook) |
  DDC 956.05/3—dc23/eng/20230603
LC record available at https://lccn.loc.gov/2023017070
LC ebook record available at https://lccn.loc.gov/2023017071

Our books may be purchased in bulk for promotional, educational, or
business use. Please contact your local bookseller or the Macmillan Corporate and
Premium Sales Department at (800) 221-7945, extension 5442, or by e-mail at
MacmillanSpecialMarkets@macmillan.com.

First Edition 2023

Designed by Kelly S. Too

Art Cartographer: Daleen Saah

Printed in the United States of America

5 7 9 10 8 6

"We do not see our hand in what happens, so we call certain events melancholy accidents when they are the inevitabilities of our projects, and we call other events necessities merely because we will not change our minds."

—Stanley Cavell

CONTENTS

CHARACTERS

PROLOGUE

Milad Salama, Abed and Haifa's son
Abed Salama, Milad's father
Haifa, Abed's wife and Milad's mother
Adam, Milad's brother
Ameen, Abed's cousin

PART ONE | THREE WEDDINGS

Ghazl Hamdan, Abed's first love
Naheel, Abed's sister and Abu Wisaam's wife
Abu Wisaam, Abed's brother-in-law
Ahmad Salama, Abed's cousin and Ameen's brother
Na'el, Abed's brother
Abu Hassan, Ghazl's father and Hassan's father
Hassan, Ghazl's brother and Abu Hassan's son
Layla, Abed's sister-in-law and Wa'el's wife
Wa'el, Abed's eldest brother
Asmahan, Abed's first wife
Lulu, Abed and Asmahan's eldest daughter

Jameela, Abed's fiancée from Kufr Kanna
Wafaa, Haifa's sister
Abu Awni, Haifa's father

PART TWO | TWO FIRES

Huda Dahbour, UNRWA doctor and Hadi's mother
Abu Faraj, UNRWA driver
Nidaa, UNRWA pharmacist
Salem, rescuer
Ula Joulani, Nour al-Houda teacher
Mustafa, Huda's father
Kamel, Huda's uncle
Ahmad Dahbour, Huda's uncle and a poet
Ismail, Huda's husband
Hadi, Huda's son

PART THREE | MASS CASUALTY INCIDENT

Radwan Tawam, bus driver
Sami, Radwan's uncle
Nader Morrar, Red Crescent paramedic
Eldad Benshtein, Mada paramedic
Dubi Weissenstern, ZAKA staff
Bentzi Oiring, ZAKA staff
Saar Tzur, IDF colonel
Tala Bahri, Nour al-Houda kindergartner
Ibrahim Salama, Abed's cousin and a PA official
Abu Mohammad Bahri, Tala's grandfather
Ashraf Qayqas, semitrailer driver

PART FOUR | THE WALL

Dany Tirza, head of IDF Rainbow Administration and architect of the wall

Beber Vanunu, founder of Adam

Adi Shpeter, Anatot resident

PART FIVE | THREE FUNERALS

Abu Jihad, Abed's cousin

Bashir, Abed's younger brother

Ruba al-Najjar, Bashir's wife

Nansy Qawasme, Salaah's mother and Azzam's wife

Azzam Dweik, Salaah's father

Salaah, Nansy and Azzam's son

Sadine, Nansy and Azzam's daughter

Fadi, Nansy's brother

Osama, Nansy's brother

Faisal, Nansy's brother

Livnat Wieder, social worker at Hadassah

Huda Ibrahim, social worker at Hadassah

Khalil Khoury, nurse at Hadassah

Haya al-Hindi, Abdullah's mother

Abdullah al-Hindi, Haya and Hafez's son

Hafez, Haya's husband and Abdullah's father

Ahmad, Abdullah's brother

EPILOGUE

Arik Weiss, Channel 10 reporter

Arik Vaknish, Adam resident

Duli Yariv, Anatot resident

A DAY IN THE LIFE
OF ABED SALAMA

Prologue

On the night before the accident, Milad Salama could hardly contain his excitement for the class trip. "Baba," he said, tugging at the arm of his father, Abed, "I want to buy food for the picnic tomorrow." They were at the apartment of Abed's in-laws, who owned a small convenience store a few steps away. Abed took his five-year-old son through one of the narrow alleys of Dahiyat a-Salaam, a neighborhood in Anata, where they lived.

On a street with no sidewalks, they inched their way between the parked cars and stalled traffic. A matrix of cables and wires and string lights hung overhead, dwarfed by the looming tower blocks that rose four, five, even six times higher than the separation barrier, the twenty-six-foot-tall concrete wall that encircled Anata. Abed remembered a time, not so long before, when Dahiyat a-Salaam was rural and bare, when it was still possible to spread out, not up. Inside the store, Abed bought Milad a bottle of the Israeli orange drink Tapuzina, a tube of Pringles, and a chocolate Kinder Egg, his favorite treat.

Early the next morning, Abed's wife, Haifa, who was slim and fair like Milad, helped the boy into his uniform: a white-collared shirt, a gray sweater bearing the emblem of his private elementary school, Nour al-Houda, and the gray pants he had to keep pulling up to his small waist. Milad's nine-year-old brother, Adam, had already left. A white school van honked lightly from the street. Milad hurried to finish his usual breakfast of olive oil, zaatar, and labneh, mopping them up with a piece of pita bread. Smiling broadly, he gathered his lunch and treats, then kissed his mother goodbye and scrambled out the door. Abed was still asleep.

When he got up, it was gray outside and raining heavily, with gusts so strong he could see people on the street struggling to walk straight. Haifa watched out the window, frowning. "The weather is not good."

"Why are you worrying like this?" Abed said, touching her shoulder.

"I don't know. Just a feeling."

Abed had the day off from his job at the Israeli phone company, Bezeq. He and his cousin Hilmi drove together to buy meat from his friend Atef, who owned a butcher shop in Dahiyat a-Salaam. Atef wasn't there, which was unusual. Abed asked one of the workers to check on him.

Atef lived in a different part of Jerusalem, Kufr Aqab, a dense urban neighborhood of tall, unregulated, and haphazardly built apartment towers that, like Dahiyat a-Salaam, was cut off from the rest of the city by a checkpoint and the wall. To avoid the daily traffic jams and the wait at the checkpoint that could last for hours, he took a circuitous route to work.

Atef reported that he was stuck in horrible traffic. There appeared to be a collision ahead of him, on the road between two checkpoints, one at the Qalandia refugee camp and the other at the village of Jaba. Moments later, Abed received a call from a nephew. "Did Milad go on the outing today? There was an accident with a school bus near Jaba."

Abed's stomach turned. He left the butcher shop with Hilmi and got into his cousin's silver jeep. They drove down the hill through the morning traffic, past the teenage boys starting work in the auto body shops with Hebrew signage for Jewish customers, past Milad's school, and then alongside the wall. The road bent around the housing developments of the Neve Yaakov settlement and climbed the steep hill to Geva Binyamin, a Jewish settlement also known as Adam, the same name as Milad's older brother.

At the Adam junction, soldiers were stopping cars from approaching the accident site, creating gridlock. Abed jumped out of the jeep. Hilmi, assuming the collision was minor, said goodbye and doubled back.

ONLY THE DAY before, Abed had nearly ruined Milad's chance to go on the trip. It was not through any sort of foresight, just inattention.

He'd been with Hilmi in Jericho, standing on the flat, dusty plain of the lowest city on Earth, hundreds of feet below sea level, when he got a call from Haifa asking if he'd paid the hundred shekels for Milad's school trip. In fact, he had forgotten. Haifa hadn't wanted Milad to go, but seeing how fervently he wanted to be with his class, she relented. Milad had been talking about the trip for days. When Haifa called, he was buzzing around her parents' home, excitedly awaiting his father's return, eager to go and buy treats. Now it was late. If Abed didn't make it to the school before it closed, Milad wouldn't be allowed on the bus the next morning.

It was midafternoon but chilly and overcast, the next day's storm starting to gather. Branches of date palms rustled in the distance. Abed told Hilmi that they had to hurry back.

Hilmi was in Jericho on business. He had recently inherited $70,000 and wanted to invest it in land. There was hardly anything left to buy in Anata, where the Salamas lived. It had once been one of the most expansive towns in the West Bank, a long strip spreading eastward from the tree-lined mountains of Jerusalem down to the pale-yellow hills and desert wadis on the outskirts of Jericho. But Israel had confiscated almost all of the land in the area or made it inaccessible to Abed and Hilmi and the people of Anata. A town of twelve square miles was now confined to less than a one-square-mile rump. So, Jericho.

Hastening to get to Milad's school in time, Abed and Hilmi drove onto Israel's main east-west thoroughfare, Highway 1. They climbed the mountain ridge, passing three gated Jewish settlements built on Anata's land and the Bedouin shantytown Khan al-Ahmar, spread over a plot owned by Abed's grandfather. Turning onto the Abu George Road, they saw the olive groves that belonged to Abed and his brothers, now taken over by settlers. Next, the route took them near the notorious E1 area where Israel planned to construct several thousand new housing units and hotel rooms, along with an industrial zone. Finally, ascending the last hill, they passed the Anatot settlement and adjacent military base, also on Salama family land.

Entering Anata, Abed and Hilmi drove to the school building, which was at the very edge of town, right up against the wall. The grounds were quiet and nearly empty. Abed ran through the metal gate and across the AstroTurf lawn to the lobby, telling the secretary he wanted to pay for the trip.

"It's too late. We're closed."

Abed rushed upstairs, finding a teacher he knew, Mufida. She called the principal, who called the secretary, and Abed went back downstairs to pay, sighing with relief. Milad would go on the trip.

IT WAS RAINING when Abed stepped out of Hilmi's SUV at the Adam junction. He was wearing the long black coat he had put on in anticipation of stormy weather. The closer he got to the site of the accident, the more anxious he became. His walk turned into a jog until he saw a green army jeep approaching. He hailed it, telling the soldiers, in Hebrew, that he thought his son was on the bus. He asked them for a lift. They refused. And now Abed started to run. He couldn't see the bus at first, his view blocked by an eighteen-wheel semitrailer stopped across two of the road's three lanes. Dozens of people were crowded together, including parents he recognized who had raced to the scene.

"Where is the bus?" Abed asked. "Where are the kids?" A moment later, he caught sight of it, flipped on its side, an empty, burned-out shell. Abed saw no children, no teachers, no ambulances. Within the crowd, he spotted a cousin he didn't very much like, Ameen. Years earlier the two had been in a vicious fight that put Abed in the hospital. Ameen now worked for the Palestinian Preventive Security Organization, which acted as Israel's enforcer in the urban centers of the West Bank. He was known to be one of the corrupt officers who shook people down.

"What happened?" Abed asked.

"Terrible accident," Ameen replied. "They carried the burned bodies out of the bus and laid them on the ground."

Abed ran from Ameen, his heart pounding. Who would tell a father something like that? This was the first Abed had heard of anyone dying. Now the dreadful image could not be erased. Abed went deeper into the crowd, Ameen's words echoing in his mind.

Rumors swirled around him, passing from one bystander to another: the kindergartners had been taken to a clinic in a-Ram, two minutes up the road; they were at Rama, the Israeli military base at the entrance to a-Ram; they were at the medical center in Ramallah; they had been transferred from Ramallah to Hadassah Hospital at Mount Scopus. Abed had to decide where to go. With his green ID from the West Bank, he would not be allowed to enter Jerusalem and check at Hadassah. The rumor about a-Ram seemed unlikely, given that it had no hospital. The medical center in Ramallah seemed most plausible. He asked two strangers for a ride. They had just traveled two and a half hours from Jenin and were headed in the opposite direction. But they agreed without hesitation.

It took a long time to inch their way out of the bumper-to-bumper traffic at the accident site. On the Jerusalem–Ramallah road they passed the play center where the class should have been by now, Kids Land. It had on its rooftop a giant SpongeBob, one of Milad's favorite cartoon characters.

Driving into Ramallah, Abed and these two kind strangers at last pulled up to the hospital, a scene of utter chaos: ambulance sirens wailing, medics wheeling injured children on gurneys, panicked parents shouting and crying, TV crews interviewing hospital staff. Pushing his way through the madness, his breath short, his chest tight, Abed tried to quell his rising terror. But his mind would not comply. Instead it fixated on one insistent thought: Am I being punished for what I did to Asmahan?

PART ONE

Three Weddings

I

Anyone who knew Abed in his youth would have told you that he was destined to end up with a certain someone. But that someone was not Haifa or Asmahan. It was a girl called Ghazl.

They met in the mid-1980s, when Anata was quiet and rural, more village than town. Ghazl was a fourteen-year-old freshman at the Anata girls' school. Abed was a senior at the boys' school across the street. Back then, everyone knew each other in Anata. More than half the village came from one of three large families all descended from the same ancestor, a man named Alawi. Abed's family, the Salamas, was the largest. Ghazl's, the Hamdans, was the second largest.

Alawi himself could trace his line back to the man who established Anata, Abdel Salaam Rifai, a descendant of the twelfth-century founder of Sufism. He had traveled from Iraq to come to al-Aqsa mosque in Jerusalem and then settled in Anata, which was perhaps named for the Canaanite goddess Anat or the biblical city Anatot. As children, Abed and his siblings would walk down the road to the old stone shrine to Abdel Salaam Rifai, lighting candles inside the domed sanctum that would later become a resting spot for Israeli soldiers, who would leave it littered with cigarette butts and beer bottles.

Abed lived a few dozen feet downhill from the girls' school, on the second floor of a two-story limestone house. The first floor served as a barn for goats, chickens, and sheep. Abed's father loved the animals, and the goats in particular. He had named each one and would beckon them to eat seeds, nuts, or sweets. As a teenager, Abed used to take the goats to graze in the small valley between Anata and Pisgat Ze'ev, a new Jewish settlement.

In Abed's youth the landscape of Anata was dotted with olive and fig trees and open fields of wheat and lentils. Large families slept together in a single room on a floor covered in thin mattresses. Homes had outhouses, and women carried water from a nearby spring in large jars balanced on their heads. Children bathed in giant buckets brought into their living rooms once a week, on Fridays, afterward lining up with wet hair and clean clothes to thank their fathers with a kiss on the hand, receiving in turn a kiss on the forehead and a blessing of comfort and bliss, *na'eeman*.

Anata began to change after Israel conquered it and the rest of the West Bank in the 1967 war. Until that point, the area had been governed by Jordan. Over the following decades, the demography and geography of the occupied territories were transformed by Israel, which used a range of policies to Judaize them. In Anata, the government seized the land piece by piece, issued hundreds of demolition orders, annexed part of the town to Jerusalem, erected a separation wall to encircle its urban center, and confiscated the rest to create four settlements, several settler outposts, a military base, and a segregated highway split down the middle by another wall, this one blocking the settlers' sight of Palestinian traffic. The town's natural pool and spring was turned into an Israeli nature reserve, which was free to the settlers of Anatot but charged admission to the people of Anata. The road to the spring went through the settlement, which Palestinians could not enter without a permit, so they had to use a different route, taking a long detour on a dangerous dirt road.

Year by year, Palestinians from Anata found themselves absorbed into the urban fabric of an expanding Jerusalem, which had swallowed up the Old City and the rest of East Jerusalem, as well as the lands of more than two dozen outlying villages, all annexed by Israel. They drove cars on Israel's multilane highways, bought food at its supermarket chains, and used Hebrew at its office towers, malls, and cinemas. But Anata's social mores remained unchanged. Prenuptial relations were forbidden, marriages were frequently arranged, and cousins coupled in order to retain wealth and land within the family. Enemies put on a show of great politeness toward one another, life outcomes were powerfully shaped by household reputation—a wayward daughter could ruin the marriage prospects of all her sisters—and the entire drama was shrouded in ritual and courteous speech.

If Anata was reminiscent of an eighteenth-century preindustrial village, Abed was born into its aristocracy. Both his grandfathers—who were brothers—had at separate points been the mukhtar, village leader, and together they had owned much of the land. But as their properties shrunk, confiscated under Israeli rule, so did the mukhtar's significance. By the early 1980s, when it was time for Abed's father to take his turn, he refused to accept the role, saying that it now consisted largely of pointing occupying soldiers to the homes of men they wanted to arrest.

Abed's father was a proud man who rarely showed resentment about the losses he had suffered, neither those of matter nor of spirit. His first love had been a woman from the Hamdan family, but his father and uncle planned for him to marry a cousin so they could avoid dividing the family's land. The parents of the girl he loved also schemed to keep the two apart because of the rivalry between the Salamas and the Hamdans. As soon as they learned of the young Salama's yearning, they married the girl off to her cousin. Abed's father was left with no choice but to respect his family's wishes and agree to the marriage they had arranged.

When Abed himself fell for a Hamdan, he wondered if he was fulfilling his father's thwarted destiny. In the evenings, he would write secret letters to Ghazl. In the mornings, he would hand them to one of her neighbors or classmates to pass to her at school. Often the notes included instructions for Ghazl to answer the phone at a certain time. Because the neighborhood she lived in, Dahiyat a-Salaam (called New Anata at the time), had been annexed by Israel and incorporated into Jerusalem, her house had a phone line. The homes in the rest of Anata did not. After school, Abed would take the bus to Damascus Gate in East Jerusalem, walk to the post office on Salahadin Street, the main commercial boulevard, and, at the arranged time, insert a token into the pay phone. The couple would speak for as long as they could, which often wasn't very long at all. If Ghazl's parents walked in, she would switch to addressing Abed in the feminine before abruptly ending the call. On many days, they barely finished saying hello before Abed found himself interrupted, midsentence, by the dull buzz of a dead phone line.

They were a handsome pair. Abed was tan and tall and svelte, with a strong jaw, a pensive gaze, and a gentle, relaxed demeanor. He had a thick head of hair, cut close at the sides, and, to his later embarrassment, a mustache. With his shirt unbuttoned low on his chest, he resembled a Palestinian James Dean. Ghazl had large, almond-shaped eyes and a dimple in her right cheek. She looked like her father. Her face, like his, radiated kindness.

Abed's oldest and favorite sister, Naheel, lived in Dahiyat a-Salaam with her husband, Abu Wisaam, in a house close to Ghazl's. From their home Abed liked to spy Ghazl on her roof or balcony, which were the only places where she would stand in the open with her hair uncovered.

Abed was secular and against the hijab. None of his sisters had worn it before they married, and Naheel didn't put one on even after. Especially among the elites, the hijab was less commonly seen. When Abed graduated from high school, in 1986, fewer than half the girls in Anata covered their hair. He didn't mind, though, that Ghazl wore the hijab. He knew she did it out of respect for her father, who was religious, and that in other ways she was far less deferential than her peers. She was also granted greater independence. Her father was amiable and trusting, and her mother—who came from Silwan, the central Jerusalem neighborhood directly beneath al-Aqsa mosque—adopted the modern ways of the city. It was their lenience that allowed Ghazl and Abed to see one another as often as they did. At least initially, before their secret courtship was able to truly flourish under the cover of joint political struggle.

THE FIRST INTIFADA broke out in December 1987, a year and a half after Abed finished high school. It began as a series of spontaneous protests that erupted when an Israel Defense Forces semitrailer collided with a station wagon in Gaza, killing four Palestinian workers. The protests spread, fueled by years of anger at what Israel's defense minister called an "iron fist policy." They quickly transformed into the first organized mass uprising against the occupation, with thousands of street battles pitting stone-throwing Palestinian youth against Israeli troops equipped with armored vehicles and assault rifles. It was a time of painful sacrifice for all Palestinians, poor and bourgeois, secular and religious, Christian and Muslim, refugee and rooted, incarcerated and expelled. With everyone suffering from Israel's determination to smash the uprising, signs of opulence and class distinction were avoided—strident secularists even adopted the hijab to show national solidarity.

Towns were besieged, curfews imposed, provisions depleted, jobs lost, schools closed, children jailed, husbands tortured, fathers killed, and sons maimed—so many bones were broken that the soldiers' clubs would snap. "The types of batons were replaced several times," according to Israel's *Kol Hazman*, "because they were too weak and broke, to the point that they were exchanged for iron batons, and when these bent, then sticks made of flexible plastic were used." More than 1,100 Palestinians were killed by Israeli soldiers or civilians during the six years of the uprising. Another 130,000 were wounded and some 120,000 were jailed. In those years, Israel had the largest per capita prison population in the world.

The Israeli military shut down all the Palestinian universities, making it impossible for Abed to get a degree. After he had finished high school, he'd hoped to study abroad. A close friend, Osama Rajabi, suggested that they apply to university in the USSR. The Palestine Liberation Organization offered scholarships in allied socialist states. Abed wanted to join Osama, but first he needed to obtain a passport, and for that he needed his father's help. Israel didn't give passports to its occupied subjects. Abed's father had a Jordanian passport, granted to him when the Hashemite Kingdom controlled the West Bank, so Abed could try to get one in

Jordan. But his father refused to help—he declared he would not allow his son to leave Palestine to become a communist. Osama left without Abed.

In Anata and elsewhere in the West Bank, the Democratic Front for the Liberation of Palestine, a Marxist-Leninist faction of the PLO, was in the vanguard of the trade union and political organizing that had given birth to the intifada. The DFLP's local leader was none other than Abu Wisaam, Abed's brother-in-law. A diminutive, witty, and loquacious intellectual, he had joined the group in the 1970s, studied in Beirut, and been trained there in espionage, explosives, and party ideology, learning about world revolutions and the Zionist movement. On a visit to Anata to see his parents, he was arrested for membership in the DFLP—an illegal organization, like all PLO factions—and during his fifteen months in jail he read the important Marxist texts. He got engaged to Naheel shortly thereafter, when she was sixteen and Abed was twelve. From that moment, Abu Wisaam had his eyes on Abed for the revolution. Once the intifada started, he recruited him to the party.

It was not just a matter of enlarging his faction's ranks. Bringing Abed into the DFLP was a way for Abu Wisaam to protect him. Rife with collaborators, Palestine had to be one of the most thoroughly penetrated societies in the history of foreign occupation and colonial rule. In the Democratic Front, at least, Abu Wisaam knew who could be trusted. On one occasion, a young member of the rival Fatah faction spread money around that he said had come from his uncle in the United States. The uncle wanted to help support the intifada, and the funds would go to buying sneakers for the *shabaab*, the youth. This was a way for the young man to begin building himself up as a leader.

He handed out five Jordanian dinars to each young activist,

enough for a pair of fresh white Nikes, the better to run in when Israeli bullets started flying. Abed took the money, but when Abu Wisaam found out, he forced him to return it right away. He knew it was a ruse: the cash had come from the Israelis, who wanted to see which of the *shabaab* were involved in the protests and who was susceptible to being bought. Every one of the boys who accepted the money was later arrested, taken from his home by Israeli soldiers in the middle of the night. Thanks to Abu Wisaam, Abed was spared.

Although most of the men in Abed's family belonged to Fatah, Yasser Arafat's party, Abed learned to distrust it. Fatah always seemed to be full of empty talk, he thought, a conviction that strengthened over the years as he watched its leaders compromise on nearly every principle, then compromise on the compromises, to the point that, after the intifada, they found themselves working as Israel's enforcers. What appealed to Abed about the Democratic Front was that on the ground, in Anata, Jerusalem, and the rest of the West Bank, the group seemed to be the most serious about building a local movement to liberate Palestine.

The DFLP supported Abed's desire to join Osama in studying law in the Soviet Union. Ghazl did, too. Abed wanted to defend the swelling ranks of Palestinian political prisoners. Every year since Osama had left, Abed asked for permission to study with him, and every year Abed's father said no.

Stuck in Anata, Abed worked in construction and rose up in the Democratic Front and its trade union, the Workers' Unity Bloc. He organized protests, recruited new members, and distributed *bayanaat*, the regular communiqués of the intifada that coordinated the actions of pharmacists, doctors, lawyers, teachers, shop owners, landlords, and local committees, providing instructions on when to strike, what to boycott, which public employees should resign, which Israeli orders should be ignored, and where to march and block transportation to the settlements. Possession of the *bayanaat*, or of any PLO "propaganda material," was a criminal offense, as was printing or publicizing "any publication of notice, poster, photo, pamphlet or other document containing material having a political significance."

The *bayanaat* had to be produced and distributed clandestinely. The means of doing so were constantly shifting, as Israel confiscated leaflets and occasionally the presses on which they were printed. Abed once obtained *bayanaat* from a young European woman who had passed through a checkpoint with the flyers hidden beneath the lining of the trunk of her car. With the broadsheets tucked under his shirt, Abed would walk to the Anata supermarket, step into an empty aisle, and scatter them across the floor. At night, he and other *shabaab* would spray-paint the texts of the *bayanaat* onto Anata's walls.

One afternoon, several weeks into the uprising, Naheel went to a DFLP demonstration at Damascus Gate. Beforehand, she had arranged an alibi. She and Abu Wisaam had been trying to have a child, and Naheel needed to take a pregnancy test. She called a clinic on Salahadin Street and scheduled an appointment for just before the protest. With the test result in hand, she joined her friends outside the Old City walls, where she began to wave the outlawed Palestinian flag. Israeli security forces pounced, but before they grabbed Naheel her friend snatched the flag out of her hand and escaped down the street. Naheel was taken to a West Jerusalem detention center in the Russian Compound area, known to Palestinians as Moscobiya. For displaying a Palestinian flag, Naheel could have been sentenced to several months or more in prison. But she hadn't been caught with the flag and was able to point to the time and date on her pregnancy test, claiming she had just been at the wrong place at the wrong time. She spent only ten days in jail.

Naheel's test was negative, but she got pregnant a little later, during the first Ramadan of the intifada. Her son was born in January 1989, a year into the uprising. When the baby was two weeks old, Abu Wisaam was arrested for his role in the DFLP. It was his third stint in an Israeli prison, and his second since marrying Naheel. This time he was jailed for almost a year. With Anata's DFLP now leaderless, Abed took over.

He spent much of that period helping Naheel with her infant son, sleeping at her house, close to Ghazl, who was then finishing her final year of high school. Abed had recruited Ghazl to the Democratic Front and now put her in charge of enlisting and educating more young women. Ghazl was good at it. There were twenty-five women active in the group when Abu Wisaam went to prison. By the time he got out, Ghazl had doubled the number.

Naheel's house near the top of the hill in Dahiyat a-Salaam offered Abed and his friends a good vantage point to spot Israeli soldiers coming up through Anata or from Shuafat refugee camp above. Shuafat Camp was a site of frequent demonstrations and one of the first Jerusalem neighborhoods put under curfew at the start of the uprising.

Abed and the people of Anata called Shuafat's residents Thawaala, the people of Beit Thul, a village near Jerusalem, because some of the largest families in the camp had been expelled from there in 1948 when Zionist forces established Israel. It was taboo to say it, because refugees were the beating heart of the Palestinian national movement—its founders, its leaders in exile, its most potent symbol, and the embodiment of the Palestinian demand to return home—but Abed did not much care for some of the Thawaala. He resented them acting as if they were the sole defenders of Palestine, somehow better than the people who had stayed on their land. He thought the camp refugees presented a false image of Palestinians as beggars, living on United Nations handouts, and they made life difficult for everyone by blocking the roads whenever there was a dispute between families.

Shuafat Camp was also a haven for drug addicts and dealers, and Abed saw Israeli soldiers there buying hash and more. Somewhere else this might have been just a social problem, but in the Palestinian context it was a national liability. Israel often recruited collaborators by threatening to expose them to their conservative families and neighbors through real or doctored photos of their transgressions, particularly sexual ones. Dealers and addicts were a source of Israeli entrapment, so they were considered a threat to the uprising. At night, Abed and other *shabaab* put on masks and started fights with the dealers, clearing potential collaborators from the streets.

INFIGHTING AMONG PALESTINIANS was one of the harshest aspects of the intifada, and it was more widespread than anyone cared to admit. Hundreds were killed and countless others were injured, Abed among them.

Ola Ja'uni, Ghazl's mentor in the Democratic Front, was a college student in charge of female recruitment and education in Jerusalem and nearby villages to the north. She attended all the protests and reported directly to the senior leadership. Abed admired Ola. She was strong, smart, and independent. Because she was also beautiful, and not from Anata—where people stared at her in the street—she attracted attention from the local Fatah *shabaab*, who heckled her when she came to town to meet Ghazl and the other DFLP activists.

One particular Fatah member went on the offensive. This was

Ahmad Salama, one of Abed's first cousins. He turned up at the Anata girls' school and disparaged Ola to the students; he then went to the homes of the girls in the Democratic Front, including Ghazl's, telling their parents that Ola was disreputable and should be kept away from their daughters. Ghazl's father defended Ola, who frequently visited the family, and threw Ahmad out of the house.

Ola was walking on Salahadin Street one day when Ahmad and a few of his Fatah friends began harassing her with crude sexual innuendo. "Hey, Ola, come with us in the car, you'll enjoy the ride!" Ola was humiliated but held her head up, first rebuking and then ignoring them as they followed her. When she got home, she told her two brothers about the heckling. That night, her brothers drove to Anata to find Ahmad. Without identifying themselves, they said they needed to talk to him about important intifada business, and Ahmad agreed to go with them. They drove a short distance to the village of Hizma, where Ola's brothers revealed their true identities and roughed him up, leaving him there.

Ahmad's injuries were mild, but he wanted revenge. He got it by telling his friends and family that he had been kidnapped and mauled by the DFLP, not mentioning his harassment of Ola or her brothers' retaliation. Now half the Salamas in Anata turned on Abed, the local head of the DFLP, wanting to know why he had ordered an attack on a family member. Abed had no idea what they were talking about and insisted the DFLP had done nothing to Ahmad. The matter was dropped, or so Abed was told.

A few months later, Abed had a visit from three DFLP members from Jerusalem who came to talk about coordinating actions for the intifada. After the meeting, Abed was walking with them to catch their Jerusalem-bound bus when Ahmad and his much larger brother, Ameen, appeared out of nowhere.

Ahmad grabbed one of Abed's visitors and accused him of

having been one of his kidnappers. Abed pulled at Ahmad's arm. "Don't talk to my guests," he said. "If you have a problem, talk to me." By now, a crowd had gathered. Abed urged his visitors to board the bus quickly and leave. "There's going to be a fight," he said, "and it has nothing to do with you."

When he turned back, Ahmad and Ameen each pulled out a knife. The three started to scuffle as people in the crowd stepped in to try to stop the fighting. Just then, Abed saw his older brother Na'el, the second-born son and black sheep of the family. Na'el had fallen in with a couple of drug dealers from Shuafat Camp and was addicted, using everything from hashish to heroin. He stole and lied, never worked, and got into fights that caused trouble with other families. He brought dealers and addicts to the Salama house, including Israelis, which prompted raids by police searching for drugs.

Na'el caused his parents great distress. They'd tried everything before Abed's father disowned him. Na'el was not his son, he said, refusing to speak to him and banishing him from eating with the family. Abed's mother would take meals to his room. She said he was sick and needed help, but Abed thought she just loved him the most. Like his father, Abed had lost all respect for Na'el. He no longer even thought of him as his older brother. Since Na'el was shunned, and Wa'el, the eldest, had lived in Jordan for many years, Abed had taken on the role of the responsible son.

Stepping out from the crowd at the bus stop, Na'el confronted Ameen as Abed and Ahmad jabbed at each other. While onlookers grabbed at their shirts, Abed struck Ahmad hard across the face, knocking him to the ground. His skull thudded against the pavement.

Meanwhile, Ameen stood menacingly over Na'el, stabbing at him. Now free, Abed approached to intervene just as Ameen

Anata and Surroundings

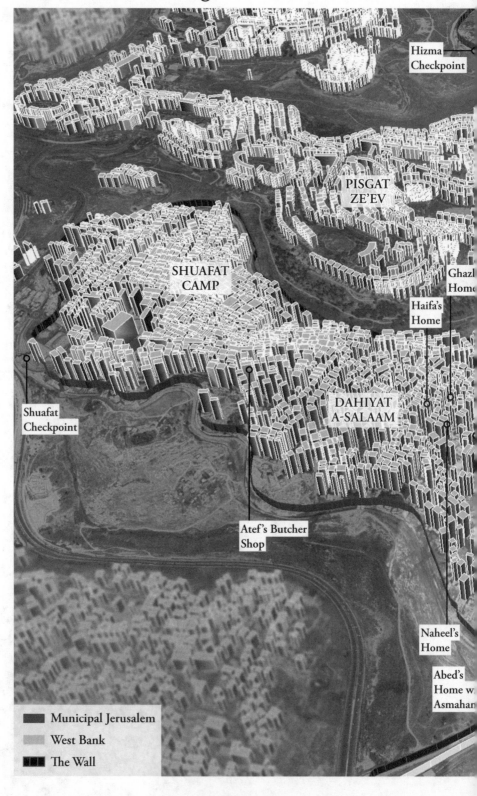

Hizma
Checkpoint

PISGAT
ZE'EV

SHUAFAT
CAMP

Ghazl
Home

Haifa's
Home

Shuafat
Checkpoint

DAHIYAT
A-SALAAM

Atef's Butcher
Shop

Naheel's
Home

Abed's
Home w
Asmahar

Municipal Jerusalem
West Bank
The Wall

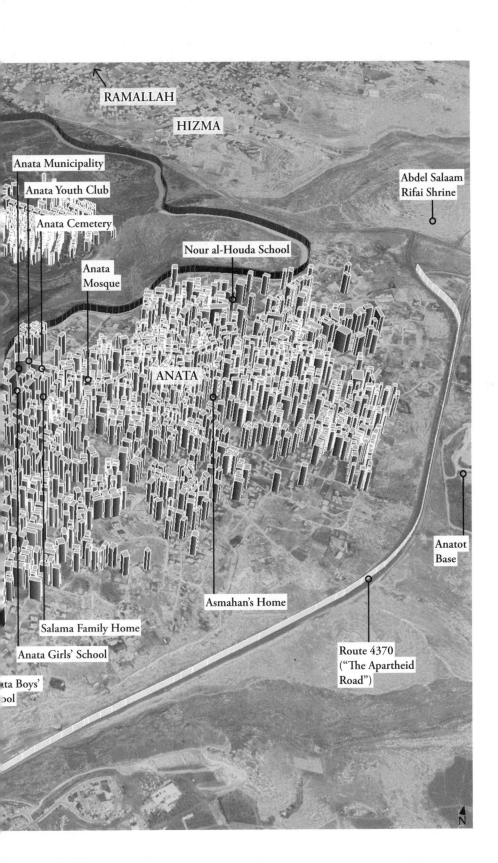

RAMALLAH

HIZMA

Anata Municipality

Anata Youth Club

Anata Cemetery

Abdel Salaam
Rifai Shrine

Nour al-Houda School

Anata
Mosque

ANATA

Anatot
Base

Asmahan's Home

Salama Family Home

Anata Girls' School

ata Boys'
ool

Route 4370
("The Apartheid
Road")

N

swung out widely, slashing Abed across his rib cage and then slicing him again on his forearm. The gashes started bleeding immediately. Seeing the blood, Ameen ran, and Na'el chased after him. Someone called an ambulance, which came from Jerusalem to take both Abed and Ahmad, who was bleeding from the blow to his head.

At Makassed Hospital, Na'el appeared at Abed's bed. "I was trying to protect you," Abed said. Na'el smiled. "Do I look like I'm hurt?" He lifted his shirt, dotted with holes from Ameen's knife, to show that he was unharmed. Na'el studied Abed's wounds, shaking his head and muttering. Then he turned to leave, saying to Abed, "Hold on." Moments later, Abed heard a great shriek, followed by shouting from down the hall. Na'el had walked into Ahmad's room, pushing past the doctor and nurses. "Excuse me," he said, before grabbing a scalpel, placing it at the point where Ahmad's jaw met his ear, and slicing down to his chin. Ahmad would have a deep, scythe-shaped scar on his face for the rest of his life. As Ahmad screamed and the staff yelled, Na'el dropped the scalpel and calmly left the room.

AFTER THE FIGHT, the elders of the Salama family arranged a *sulha*, a traditional process of reconciliation, between Abed's family and Ahmad's. Each side had one injured son, so no reparations were required. Abed refused to attend: he had done nothing wrong, whereas Ahmad had harassed Ola, falsely accused the DFLP of beating him, and attacked Abed without cause. By excluding himself from the *sulha*, Abed was preserving the right to exact revenge. But his seniors in the Democratic Front told him to let it go: Palestinians were supposed to be fighting the Israelis, not each other. Ahmad's family received compensation for the beating by Ola's brothers, and the Democratic Front covered Abed's medical bills.

When Abed returned home from the hospital, Ghazl paid him a visit. She had cut class and walked down the hill to see him. Abed's parents greeted her and left the two alone together. But Abed's father was unhappy, and later he reprimanded Abed. "What if someone like Ameen saw her come here alone? What if he told her father? What would her parents say?" Ghazl could be punished or beaten. Her father could turn against Abed. He and Ghazl could ruin their chances of being together, or even of marrying well, by endangering themselves this way.

Abed was reclining on a bed his parents had brought into the living room. He lay on one side to ease the pressure on his ribs. Ghazl sat on a divan close by. She asked after his health and then pointed to his chest. "Where's your necklace?" she said. Abed reached up and felt that it was missing. "Sorry," he said, "I must've lost it in the fight. I'll buy another one." Ghazl and Abed had been wearing matching silver necklaces for years. They both had medallions with the first letters of their names in English transliteration of the Arabic. Ghazl's had an *A* for the *ayn* in Abed's name; Abed's had a *GH* for the *ghayn* in Ghazl's. In Arabic the two letters were nearly identical, distinguished only by a single dot.

Ghazl had news for Abed. After the fight, she had been sitting on her porch, talking with her four sisters and a cousin. She didn't yet know the extent of Abed's injuries and was worried. One of her aunts happened to approach and said she had found a necklace. The girls, all close in age, began to clamor for it. "I want it!" "No, me!" "Me!" But Ghazl's aunt had already decided who should have it. "This is for Ghazl," she said, handing it over. She knew nothing about the matching necklaces and had no inkling that the one she had found belonged to Abed. She simply thought a *GH* necklace should go to Ghazl.

"Where did you find it?" Ghazl asked her aunt.

"On the street below my house."

Ghazl knew who it belonged to.

Now Ghazl pulled the necklace out of her pocket, placed it in Abed's palm, and for a heart-stopping moment held her delicate fingers against his hand. It was the only time they touched.

II

Abed's work in the DFLP inevitably drew the attention of the Israelis. In the fall of 1989, almost two years after the start of the intifada and nine months into Abu Wisaam's jail sentence, soldiers came to Abed's home one night. Blindfolded and with his hands zip-tied behind him, he was thrown into the back of an army truck with half a dozen other detainees, all sitting on the cold, hard bed of the vehicle, bent forward over their crossed legs. Then the blindfolds were removed. Abed recognized the other young men: three were from the DFLP and three from Fatah. As the truck made its way to the detention center in Ramallah, two soldiers in the back beat and cursed Abed and the rest of the handcuffed detainees, then took turns hurling themselves at their heads.

Abed and his comrades were put in a large tent next to the Ramallah jail, which was an old Tegart fort, a type of building erected during the 1936–39 Arab Revolt against the British Mandatory authorities. Named after their designer, Sir Charles Tegart, a colonial police officer, they were later used by Israel as jails and police stations. Once the soldiers had left, the Fatah detainees interrogated the prisoner they suspected had turned them in. It was the same Fatah activist who had handed out five Jordanian dinars to the *shabaab* before they were rounded up. Israel often arrested its own informants, so that they could avoid suspicion and also continue to gather intelligence from inside the jails. After the others beat him, the Fatah activist confessed to having given their names to Israel in exchange for thirty-five shekels, roughly forty dollars.

From the Ramallah tent Abed was transferred to an unsanitary facility south of Hebron, Dhahiriya, where he was interrogated. The plainclothes captains of Israel's intelligence service, the Shabak, tortured him in the usual method, known as *shabih,* a reference to the stretching of the prisoners' arms. A filthy, putrid sack was placed over his head, and his hands were shackled to a pipe high above him so that only his toes touched the ground, pulling his limbs as if on a vertical rack. Unlike some of the detainees, who endured *shabih* for an entire day, Abed's torture ended after an hour. The Israelis didn't need him to confess: they said two members of his cell had already given him up as their leader.

Abed hired one of the most prominent Israeli Jewish lawyers representing Palestinians, Lea Tsemel. A sharp-witted forty-four-year-old who looked something like a pixie, with sparkling green eyes and short brown hair, she had spent nearly two decades waging a quixotic battle against the laws and military orders that denied Palestinians their basic civil rights. She explained to Abed that under the Tamir Amendment—named for an Israeli justice minister who had commanded the bombing of the British tax offices in Jerusalem in 1944—he could be convicted solely on the basis of a statement by a third party, without the right to cross-examine or even demand the appearance of this person in court.

After his interrogation, Abed was sent to the Ofer prison

near Ramallah, then to a detention facility in the Anatot base, which, as it happened, was built on land confiscated from his family. Detainees used buckets as toilets. Abed stayed there for two months and was allowed to shower only twice. Next he went back to Ofer, where he was tried and sentenced by a military court to six months, then to Dhahiriya again, and finally out of the West Bank to Israel's largest prison, Ketziot, in the Negev Desert. It was built to confine the thousands of West Bank and Gaza Palestinians rounded up during the intifada, at a certain point holding one in every fifty Palestinian men. Politically aware inmates named it Ansar III, after the Ansar prison camp Israel had erected when it occupied Southern Lebanon. But most referred to it by the Arabic name for the area since before Israel colonized it, the Naqab.

Abed arrived in the Naqab in the winter, when the temperature of the desert nights would drop below freezing. The facility was made up of more than one hundred crowded tents, with a couple dozen detainees in each. Every cluster of two to four tents was surrounded by a dirt mound and enclosed with barbed wire. It was easier for Israel to control the inmates by giving some autonomy to the factions, allowing each to run its own tent. In Abed's cluster, there was one tent for the DFLP, one for Fatah, and one for the Islamists. When new prisoners were brought in, they would line up before the heads of the factions and declare their party affiliation. Not everyone had one, so this was the moment when they had to decide.

Abed saw one prisoner approach the front of the line and declare, "I'm with the PLO." Everyone around him laughed. "We're all PLO!" one of the party leaders said, since the PLO was not a faction but the umbrella group for all the non-Islamist parties. "Okay, I'm with Abu Ammar," the man offered, using the *kunya*, or honorific, for Yasser Arafat. He was put with Fatah.

Two months later, Abed saw that this man, who had not known the name of the faction he joined, was now the head of Fatah education in his cluster. That, Abed thought, is how they choose their leaders.

At the time, nearly half of the thirteen thousand Palestinians in Israeli jails were in the Naqab. The inmates included most of the more than two thousand Palestinians held under administrative detention—that is, held without having been charged or tried and with the possibility that their sentence might be extended indefinitely. Among them were journalists, attorneys, physicians, professors, students, trade unionists, civil society leaders, advocates of nonviolence, and members of Israeli-PLO dialogue groups, which were illegal. Unlike Abed, most were not told the reason for their imprisonment.

Each tent set its own daily schedule. Abed's DFLP tent held mandatory courses in party objectives, policies, and ideology, and instruction on how to withstand interrogation by the Shabak. Some inmates read and translated newspaper articles brought in by their lawyers. Televisions and radios were forbidden, great numbers of books were banned—from Shakespeare, Tolkien, and Tolstoy to Solzhenitsyn and *The Constitutional Law of the State of Israel*—and none of the prisoners was allowed a family visit.

The tents had no tables or chairs, and they flooded when it rained. Even during dust and sandstorms the soldiers required the tent flaps to remain open. The barrels used for trash overflowed each day, bringing a terrible stench and an influx of mosquitoes and rats. Many prisoners developed skin diseases. But the real torment came at sunset. Every night the Israelis would turn on the speakers and play a heartrending ballad by Umm Kulthum. She was Abed's favorite singer, along with Abdel Halim Hafez; he disliked pop music and listened only to the classics. The Israelis played a different wrenching Umm Kulthum song each night. Her songs were lengthy; the most famous, "Enta Omri" ("You Are My Life"), was almost an hour long. The anguished prisoners would lie on their beds listening, homesick, some of them crying, others working on the one letter they were allowed to send each month. Abed didn't dare try to write to Ghazl. The Israelis read all the mail, and who knew how they would use the information against him. Or her. Instead, he would stand outside the tent and look up at the moon, wondering if at that moment Ghazl was looking at it, too.

III

Upon his release, Abed received a new ID card, colored green to identify him as a former prisoner. Standard West Bank ID cards were orange, but ex-detainees were given green ones for different lengths of time, depending on how long they had served and for what. Abed's was for six months. It was an effective means of constraining him even after he had finished his sentence. He was turned away at checkpoints whenever he showed the green ID. Sometimes he was treated roughly or beaten. He gave up trying to leave Anata, resigning himself to another six-month stretch.

The different-colored ID cards were a fairly new means of regulating the movement of Palestinians from the occupied territories. From the early years of Israeli rule, a blanket military order had allowed them to move quite freely in the West Bank, Gaza, East Jerusalem, and pre-1967 Israel. Unless there was a general closure of the territories, a Palestinian could have breakfast in Ramallah, lunch in Jerusalem, and dinner in Haifa as long as he returned home by 1:00 A.M.

That changed during the intifada, with the emergence of an

ever-more labyrinthine system of restrictions. Israel put up check-points within the occupied territories, along the pre-1967 lines, and between East Jerusalem and the West Bank. The ability to pass through them depended on the color of your ID, what part of the occupied territories you were born in, how old you were, your gender, and whether you had ever been detained or arrested.

The green IDs took on a different meaning a few years later. The costs of the intifada had convinced Israel that it would be easier to govern the occupied territories through an intermediary. To that end, Israel allowed the PLO's exiled leadership to return to Palestine to head limited self-rule in the occupied urban areas. Israel maintained control over the population registry and the permit system, deciding who could enter, leave, and reside in which parts of the territory, but it gave the newly created Palestinian Authority the symbolic role of issuing Israeli-approved ID cards. For West Bank residents, the PA chose to switch the orange cards to green, the old color for ex-prisoners. Abed thought it fitting; every Palestinian was a sort of prisoner, from the youngest child to the PA president, who also needed Israel's permission to come and go.

Post-prison confinement in Anata wasn't all bad, though. Abed resumed his position as local leader of the Democratic Front. The intifada was still going strong. As soon as he got back his orange ID, which allowed him to enter Jerusalem, Abed took a job with Ghazl's father, Abu Hassan, a successful contractor who worked mostly on Israeli projects in the city, where the pay was much higher than in Anata. Abed spent every workday with Ghazl's father and Hassan, her older brother. They grew close. Abed addressed Abu Hassan as "Uncle," a gesture of affection and respect. One of Ghazl's younger brothers, who occasionally worked alongside them and had been recruited to the DFLP by his sister, became a dear and lifelong friend.

Abed didn't like to work for Israelis, particularly in the settlements, but he endured it to strengthen his relationship with Abu Hassan. They built houses across the city: in the East Jerusalem settlement of Pisgat Ze'ev; in upscale Qatamon, the prosperous, formerly Christian Palestinian neighborhood that had been home to some of the refugees now living in Shuafat Camp; and in the ultra-Orthodox neighborhood of Bucharim, where they built a synagogue for one of the most popular rabbis in Israel, Yitzhak Kaduri, a Baghdad-born Kabbalist who distributed amulets promising his followers health and prosperity.

Abed hadn't given up on his hope of going to law school in the USSR. After several failed attempts to convince his father, he finally decided on a new approach. He went to his father's friends and begged them to speak with him. "He has no reason to deny me anymore. I'm already a communist." Abed's father relented. But as the paperwork was being processed the Soviet Union collapsed. Abed would never get a degree.

In his spare time, he worked on the single-story home he had begun building just before his arrest, where he planned to start a family with Ghazl. A short walk up the hill from her parents' place, it was on his grandfather's land at the top of Dahiyat a-Salaam, with clear eastern views all the way to the Dead Sea. A shared life in that home was as much Ghazl's dream as his. For years they had met furtively to go over the blueprints and plot their future, choosing the location of the kitchen, the living room, the bedroom.

By this point, the two had been together for seven years. Abed was twenty-three and Ghazl twenty-one, now a nursing student. Their relationship was still secret, at least as far as Ghazl's family was concerned. But they were so often in one another's company, so clearly in love, that many people knew. Abed's parents mostly turned a blind eye, even as the couple had started to raise a few eyebrows. It was only a matter of time before Ghazl's parents would find out. Her brother Hassan had already started to grow suspicious. One day he demanded to know why she wore an *A* necklace and Abed one with *GH*. Ghazl said she had no idea what Abed wore, but her necklace was for her older sister, Abeer. Eventually Abed's father told him it was unacceptable to carry on this way with a girl he hadn't married. "This isn't our ethics," he said. "If you want to marry her, you have my permission."

Abed decided to propose. He told Naheel, and within minutes they were walking the short distance to Ghazl's house. Abed sat with Hassan and asked for her hand, while Naheel spoke with Ghazl's mother in another room. Hassan and Ghazl's mother thanked them and said they would need two to three days to consult with the family.

At the construction site early the next morning, Abed asked Hassan for news. Hassan said he had talked to his father, who needed to speak with Ghazl's grandfather. He promised that Abed would have his answer in a day.

As it happened, Abed saw Abu Hassan that same afternoon. Abed had been enlisted to help his sister-in-law Layla with the construction of her house. Layla was married to Wa'el, Abed's oldest brother. She had grown up in Anata but had only recently moved back from Jordan, where she and Wa'el and their two young daughters had been living for several years. Weeks after Abed's release from prison, Wa'el had been arrested at the Allenby Bridge as he crossed from Jordan to the West Bank. He had told

Layla he was going home for a visit. When she didn't hear from him, she called her family in Anata. No one knew where Wa'el was until Abed's parents contacted the International Committee of the Red Cross and learned of his arrest at the border.

Just before Wa'el had left for his trip, an ex-Israeli soldier named Ami Popper had got up early in the morning, put on his brother's IDF pants, grabbed his brother's Galil assault rifle, and walked to a bus stop in the town of Rishon Letzion. Laborers from Gaza were waiting there for Israeli employers to pick them up. Pretending to be an officer, Popper asked the workers for their IDs and ordered them to line up in rows and kneel. When a car with Gaza license plates approached, he told the driver to stop and get out with all his passengers. He then opened fire, slaughtering seven and severely injuring eleven more.

Wa'el was incensed. He met a contact in Fatah and proposed to avenge the murders by attacking a target in annexed East Jerusalem, the national police headquarters at Israel's government complex in Sheikh Jarrah. The plan was for him to cross the border, return to Anata, and pick up explosives from a hidden location. He was to rig them to a vehicle and park it at the police headquarters before detonating it from afar. Arriving at the Allenby Bridge nine days after the massacre, Wa'el was arrested without being told the charges.

He spent several hours waiting in a small room before being driven to the Moscobiya detention facility, from which he was transferred to Ramallah a day later. Eventually, he was taken to see an officer. "Welcome to the one who came to fuck Israel," the officer said in Arabic. "We're honored to have you." For eleven days of interrogation, the Shabak operatives asked why Wa'el had tried to return to Anata. He stuck to his story: he came to pick up his mother and father to take them on the upcoming hajj, the annual pilgrimage to Mecca. The interrogators slammed him against a wall, shook him violently, and threatened to arrest his wife, but they never specified the charges. If he didn't confess, they said, he would get fifteen to twenty years in prison.

After the eleven days, he was taken with another detainee to a new cell. The prisoners there were all from Fatah. They greeted Wa'el and his fellow detainee, gave them food, and showed them the showers. Wa'el hadn't bathed since his arrest. In the cell there were many books about the Palestinian revolution, and he felt relieved to be among comrades. After the sunset prayer, a prisoner with a large beard said they were all brothers and they would provide whatever he might need. On visitors' day, he said, they could smuggle letters out for Wa'el.

Since his arrest, Wa'el had been worried that someone might find the hidden explosives and get hurt. So he wrote a letter to the Fatah military leadership, warning of the danger, and gave it to the bearded prisoner. When Wa'el was sent back for interrogation the next morning, he realized he had been duped. Everyone in the cell was an *asfour*, a bird, slang for a prison collaborator. Israel now had its charges.

Wa'el was sentenced to eight years. Layla and their two daughters moved back to Anata and lived with her parents, close to Abed's home. Abed's family stepped in to help raise the children, the elder of whom was just three years old when Wa'el went to jail. Abed doted on his young nieces, buying them gifts and taking them on frequent trips to Jerusalem playgrounds and the Old City. He and his brothers made plans to build a house for Wa'el and his family when he got out of prison. The plans had gained steam at the time of Abed's proposal to Ghazl, and the Salamas were ready to hire a contractor. Layla and Abed had arranged to speak to Ghazl's uncle about the job. He had built a number of homes in town. Unlike Abu Hassan, he worked primarily for Palestinians.

Layla drove Abed up the hill in her tiny red Fiat to see Ghazl's uncle, who lived next door to the rest of the family. As they reached his house, Abed spotted Ghazl on her second-floor balcony. He beamed at the sight. Getting out of the car, Layla said that she could ask Abu Hassan, who was her first cousin, how he intended to respond to Abed's proposal. She was close to the family and could put in a good word for Abed, she said. Layla was known to be a meddler, so he declined the offer, asking her to please stay out of it—they would give him their answer in the next few days. Layla agreed.

At the house, they found Ghazl's uncle, a neighbor, and Abu Hassan. Layla left them to join the women in another room. The men discussed the construction project, and Ghazl's uncle promised to get back to Abed with an estimate. Abu Hassan then went out of the room for a moment to do *wudu*, the ablutions of face, arms, head, and feet before prayer, and Abed left with Layla a short time later.

On the way to the car, as Ghazl looked down on them from the balcony, Layla confessed that she had spoken to Abu Hassan when he had left the room for *wudu*. Abed angrily reminded her that she had promised not to intervene. She hadn't meant to, she said; it was Abu Hassan who had initiated the conversation.

"So," Abed asked, testily. "What did he say?"

With an air of solicitude that was not entirely convincing, Layla relayed the exchange. "Abed is a good guy," Ghazl's father had reportedly said, "a hard worker. He's strong, affable, funny. I've gotten to know him well. But there's one thing I can't accept: he's a Salama." Layla saw the shock and pain on Abed's face.

"Really? He said that?"

"Yes," Layla said, with cloying sympathy. "He did."

Abed was blinded by the intensity of his humiliation. Though faintly aware that his reaction was precisely what Layla hoped to see, he was unable to quash his anger.

"You tell him that I withdraw the proposal!" Turning to face Ghazl, who was still out on the balcony, he added, "Ghazl is like a sister to me and I could never marry her." He wasn't sure if Ghazl had heard him.

At the construction site the next day, Abed avoided Hassan and Abu Hassan. All morning and afternoon he could sense them watching him, lingering nearby, looking for an opening. But he averted his gaze and moved away when either one approached. Nothing was said about the proposal. After work, Abed kept his distance from Ghazl, too. He didn't call or visit or send word. Ghazl was used to seeing him every afternoon, but days passed with no contact. He heard through friends and relatives that she was distraught. Then her sister relayed a message through Abed's brother: Ghazl had to see him, as soon as possible.

They arranged to meet at Ghazl's nursing college near Kufr Aqab. He expected they would talk on the grounds of the campus, but Ghazl insisted that they take a bus to downtown East Jerusalem, where they would have more privacy. There was a strike that day—strikes were still common at this point in the intifada, now in its fifth year—so all the cafés and restaurants were closed. They got off the bus near Damascus Gate and walked to the East Jerusalem YMCA, next door to an old stone villa belonging to the US consulate. They sat outside on the steps of the YMCA, facing its garden.

"What did you do? What happened?" Ghazl asked. "A man is supposed to come back after he proposes and ask for an answer."

"I'm sorry, but we can't continue," Abed said. "Your father

doesn't like the Salamas. He's ashamed to be associated with us," he spat out. "I'm not ashamed. I'm proud to be a Salama." He paused, looking out at the winding pathway lined with palm and cypress trees, thinking first of the home they planned to build, then of Abu Hassan's insult. "Ghazl, you're like a sister to me. I can't marry you."

Ghazl began to cry and then shout. "I don't understand," she said, her eyes searching his. "I don't understand."

On the bus back to Anata, they sat separately. There were too many people on it who knew them. Abed watched Ghazl cry all the way from Damascus Gate to her stop in Dahiyat a-Salaam.

IV

Abed was in a fragile state. His dreams for the future were in ruins. He got off the bus and wandered the streets, agitated and confused, shaken by Ghazl's tears and bewilderment. At times like these, the person he most wanted to see was Naheel. He walked to her place and sat on her steps. Ghazl was out on her balcony, hunched over the balustrade, her head resting on her forearms. They didn't acknowledge each other.

Naheel and Abu Wisaam joined Abed on the steps. They had never seen him so forlorn. Wanting to console him, Naheel said that he would find someone else, someone better. She went inside to put the kettle on and came back out with a photo of a girl who was about Abed's age. Handing it to him, Naheel asked if he recognized her. He said he had never seen her before.

"She's your cousin," Naheel said.

"Whose cousin?"

"Yours! The daughter of Abu Wisaam's brother. You don't recognize her?"

Abed examined the snapshot closely, not that it mattered much. He was too wretched to care or even notice that the young woman was pretty, petite, with caramel skin and large eyes. He barely registered that she was a Salama. In fact, she was also Ghazl's first cousin on her mother's side. Naheel said she was kind, dutiful, a good girl. Her name was Asmahan. "If you want, we can arrange an engagement right now."

Abed was enraged by Abu Hassan and angry at himself for being stupid enough to fall for a Hamdan, a girl whose father held the Salamas in contempt. His father had made the same mistake. Abed wanted to punish Abu Hassan, punish Ghazl and himself. In his anguish, he was unable to calm himself or think clearly. He wanted to blot out the jilted girl on her balcony, to erase his grief, to escape. His sister was offering a way out. Presented with a life-changing proposition, he gave it scarcely a moment's thought. He said okay.

Abu Wisaam offered to go see his brother and tell him that Abed was on his way to propose. He instructed Naheel to take Abed to their parents' house. Abed's father listened impassively to the news and offered no congratulations. "What about Ghazl?" he asked. Abed didn't want to entangle his father in a dispute with Abu Hassan so he said nothing about why he had changed his mind. He no longer desired Ghazl, he said.

Abed's father tried again. "You went to their house and spoke to her family." This was as close as anyone came to suggesting that Abed not give up on the girl he had loved for seven years. No one told him he was acting hastily. No one advised him to wait a few days.

"It's over, *khalas*," finished, Abed said. "I don't want her."

His father kept quiet. After a while, he said, "It's your choice, your life."

Together Abed and Naheel and their parents went to see Asmahan's family in Dahiyat a-Salaam. Abu Wisaam had gone ahead and spoken to her father, who had given his consent. In the living room, Abed sat with his parents, Abu Wisaam, and Asmahan's father, brothers, uncle, and a neighbor who was close to the family. The women—Asmahan, her mother, her sisters, and Naheel—were in the next room.

Observing the formalities, Abed's father made the proposal, and Asmahan's father respectfully accepted it. In both rooms, everyone whispered the Fatiha, the seven-verse prayer that opens the Quran. Less than two hours had elapsed from the moment Naheel had shown Abed the photo.

The next day Abed went with his father and Asmahan's mother to the goldsmiths' souk, near the Church of the Holy Sepulchre in the Old City, and bought a silver ring for himself and a gold ring and other jewelry for Asmahan. Soon after, the families held an engagement party at Asmahan's home, with more than a hundred people attending. The women danced in the living room; outside on the front patio, the men sat on plastic chairs and talked. When all the guests had arrived, Abed's father stood up and announced the proposal on behalf of the family. "We have come here to ask your daughter to marry our son." Asmahan's father accepted, and the men held their cupped hands before their faces, looking downward, to recite the Fatiha. Then they congratulated Abed while the women ululated and cheered in the living room. Abed shook the hand of every man there as *baklawa* and glasses of cola were passed around.

Asmahan's father took Abed inside. They walked past the women and girls—some fifty sisters, cousins, mothers, aunts, grandmothers, and neighbors—and stopped at a table with two chairs on it. Asmahan was standing on the table wearing a pink gown, her hair arranged glamorously; Abed, in a black suit, got up on the table to join her. One of Abed's sisters held out a box with the gold ring, necklace, earrings, watch, and bracelet that Abed would place on his fiancée. She in turn would put the silver ring on Abed, then they would sit on the chairs atop the table and the women would dance around them.

As he put the gold ring on Asmahan's finger, Abed heard a commotion. With dozens of women staring at him, he was too nervous to look for the source of the noise. It was Ghazl. She had run from the room, tears spilling from her eyes, as two cousins chased after her. A bedroom door slammed shut. Abed hadn't seen her leave—he hadn't even known she was there. If he had, he might have run after her.

Had Ghazl stayed home, her relatives might have guessed that she was still attached to Abed. She felt compelled to attend and put on a display of stoic indifference. Instead, she had made a scene in front of all the women, falling apart when Abed came into the room. As he stood on the table, her cousins whispered that she mustn't let anyone see her distress. A moment later, Abed put the ring on Asmahan and Ghazl fled the ceremony.

She got engaged several weeks later, accepting the proposal of a young Fatah man who lived next door. In one of her old letters to Abed, she had written that of all the people in Anata, she hated this man the most. Her friend Khulood told her to give Abed another chance. It wasn't too late. Abed was merely engaged, not married. He might still return to her. They had been together for so long, Ghazl shouldn't lose hope. The man who had proposed to her—though intelligent and educated, a mathematics teacher—was not the one she wanted, not an adequate match.

Khulood's brother, who was friends with Abed, reported Ghazl's reply. She had accepted the proposal not because of her neighbor's character but because of his mind. In any case, Abed was now engaged, and she couldn't go back to him. He had said she was like his sister. *Khalas*, it was finished.

There were many times over the years when Abed thought how it all could have been so different. If only Ghazl had listened to Khulood. If only someone had given him the same advice. Calling off an engagement was hardly a scandal. It happened all the time. If he and Ghazl had reunited, everyone would have understood. Even Asmahan and her parents, who knew about their relationship. He blamed Naheel as well. She shouldn't have shown him the picture of Asmahan, shouldn't have talked about another girl. At that moment, he would have agreed to marry anyone. She had taken advantage of his vulnerability, he thought.

Not until two decades later—after Ghazl had children, after Abed and Haifa had their boys—did Abed learn who was to blame. He was with Abu Hassan at the Anata iron factory, sitting outside, drinking coffee, listening to him tell an old story. When Abu Hassan reached the punch line, he smiled broadly. Abed loved that smile.

"Uncle," he said, "I want to ask you something that's been eating away at me. Do you remember when I proposed to Ghazl?"

"Yes, and you didn't come back."

"I want to tell you why." Abed recounted what Layla had told him.

Abu Hassan got up angrily from his chair. "I said that? I never said that! I'll go to Layla right now!"

Abed wasn't surprised. He had suspected that Layla had lied to him. Now that Abu Hassan confirmed it, he felt a shaft of remorse. He had allowed his pride to upend his life and Ghazl's. If he had only approached her father, he and Ghazl would have been together. Abed calmed Abu Hassan and said it no longer mattered. It wasn't meant to be.

Abed and Asmahan were married a year after their engagement. Although Abed had been the first to propose, Ghazl's wedding took place before his. Their paths would often cross in Anata, but neither one would speak. Ghazl blushed when she passed Abed, her cheeks turning so pink he could see them change color even as she drove by. When she looked at him directly, Abed saw the blame in her mournful eyes. Long after they had split, long after they had started families, the accusation was still there. It was he who had caused her to live this life, he who had wrecked the one they had planned.

V

Abed and Ghazl both married in 1993, the year Israel and the PLO signed the Oslo Accords, which brought an end to the intifada and led to the formation of the Palestinian Authority, the *sulta*, with its limited self-governing powers in the most heavily populated pockets of Gaza and the West Bank.

Ghazl and her husband were employed in the *sulta*'s Education Ministry in Ramallah. One year, toward the end of the second semester, Abed showed up at her office. His nephew was preparing to graduate high school and take the final set of exams, the *tawjihi*. He had recently undergone surgery in Jordan for a brain tumor. The operation was successful but had left him with severely impaired vision that his doctors believed would eventually improve. At that moment, however, he could not see well enough to complete the *tawjihi*. Abed's sister asked him to look into the possibility of special testing.

Abed went to Ramallah, stopping at a pay phone in Clock Tower Square to call the ministry. A secretary gave him the number for the Department of School Health. When he called, he heard a familiar voice.

"Hello, *marhaba*," a woman said.

Abed didn't answer.

"*Ahlan*, hello," the woman said again.

"One second," Abed replied. "I know you."

"Who is this?" she asked.

Abed paused. "Is this Ghazl?"

"Yes," she said slowly, before recognizing him, too. "Ah, Abed." They had not spoken since that day on the steps of the YMCA.

"I need to speak to you about my nephew. Where's your office?"

Abed arrived a few minutes later. A receptionist pointed him to Ghazl's department. One room was empty; a man sat in the second. Ghazl had gone to the bathroom, the man said, and would be back shortly. Abed should wait.

When Ghazl appeared, her eyes were puffy and red. It was clear she had been crying. Another employee came to join them in her office, adding to the tension and awkward formality. Abed apologized for bothering Ghazl and then described his nephew's situation. He could see how she was suffering in his presence, stammering at first and then speaking with evident difficulty. But she promised to do her best to help the boy. Abed regretted causing her discomfort. He had underestimated how hard the encounter would be for him, too. Hastening to end it, he thanked her, saying he wouldn't be able to return to the ministry. She should be in touch with the boy's parents.

Abed found himself thinking of her constantly. His preoccupation was obvious to everyone around him, including Asmahan. It wasn't that he didn't love his wife. She was beautiful, kind, and attentive, a skilled cook, and a devoted mother to their daughter, Manolia, whom they called Lulu, born a year and a half after the wedding. His mother and sisters also loved Asmahan. She was, in their view, an ideal wife. But no matter how much his family praised her, she wasn't enough. He wanted more than a good mother, a good cook, more even than beauty. Asmahan was a wife and a companion. She was not a lover or a partner.

Abed felt as though he had inherited the failures of his father, who had also lost his soul mate and wound up with a woman that he couldn't love in the same way. His father, too, was content enough in his marriage but not fulfilled. Abed had always seen his parents as opposites, his father's character as strong as his mother's was weak. His relationship with Asmahan was the same. She couldn't make a decision about the simplest things. No matter what Abed asked, the answer was always some variant of "Whatever you like." How different it would have been with Ghazl.

He reminded himself that none of this was Asmahan's fault. He had chosen her, not the other way around. She was innocent and even sympathetic to Abed's longing for Ghazl. They spoke about it openly. If anyone mentioned Ghazl's name, Abed's head would turn. When Abed's parents and siblings told a love story or watched a romantic film, they looked at him searchingly. So did Asmahan. "I hope the day will come when you say you love me more than Ghazl," she once told him. She said it earnestly, without bitterness.

Abed was racked with guilt. She didn't deserve to be treated this way, to be an object her husband sought to escape. He stayed out of the house as much as he could. He had left construction work and taken on two jobs, one at Israel's telephone company, Bezeq, and one as a cook at Askadinya, a Sheikh Jarrah restaurant named after the loquat tree in its dining room. Abed worked at Bezeq until the afternoon, overseeing a crew of repairmen fixing telephone lines all over East Jerusalem, from Dahiyat a-Salaam and Shuafat Camp to the Mount of Olives and the Old City. He would come home for a quick shower, change his clothes, and leave for the restaurant.

He wouldn't return until after midnight. When Abed's shift ended, he would go out with his friend Midhat, the chef at Askadinya. Midhat had taught Abed to cook, bringing him up from dishwasher to sous-chef in just a few months. They'd walk along the Tayelet, the promenade built on land Israel had confiscated from Jabal Mukaber, taking in the cool night air and the sweeping views of the Old City with the golden Dome of the Rock lit up at its center. Or they'd go to Musrara, the neighborhood near Damascus Gate, and buy some freshly baked Jerusalem *ka'ek*, ring-shaped sesame bread, and take it back to the staff at Askadinya. No matter how late Abed stayed out, Asmahan would be waiting with the dinner she had made. It was the only time she had with him. Even this he sometimes ruined by bringing Midhat home with him, and still Asmahan would graciously serve them her *maqluba*, *musakhan*, or *mansaf*. Abed recognized that it was a horrible life for her. She suffered it quietly, rarely complaining.

After the birth of their second daughter, Fatima, whom they called Fufu, Abed began to think of taking another wife. According to Jordanian law, which remained in effect in the family courts in East Jerusalem, he was allowed to have four. None of the men in his or his father's generation had more than one wife, and he would surely encounter stiff resistance, perhaps ostracism, from the women of Anata, who wouldn't want their husbands and sons to follow suit. But he was willing to pay the price. He desperately needed a change. Marrying Asmahan had ruined his life and hers, as well as Ghazl's. Maybe he deserved to be punished for his mistake, but not with a life sentence, he reasoned.

He never considered a divorce. He wanted to do right by Asmahan, or as right as he could under the circumstances, and divorce would have meant her returning to her childhood home and living under her parents' thumb or separating from her children if she remarried. His plan was to continue to support her, for her and their daughters to live in his family home, and to bring his new wife to his house in Dahiyat a-Salaam. He thought he would spend three nights a week with Asmahan and four with his second wife. Asmahan wouldn't be happy about it, but she was miserable now. They both were.

Abed floated the idea of marrying again. He mentioned it in front of Asmahan's parents, who appeared to think he was joking. He raised it with Asmahan, who seemed to be guided by the maxim of Anata's older women: bring a husband many children and he will never leave you. She had just given birth to their third daughter, all in the space of three and a half years. Abed told her he wanted them to take a break. He was working two jobs with a newborn, a toddler, and a small child at home. But just a year later, she called him from the doctor's office to say she was pregnant again. He hung up the phone at Askadinya and stormed through the kitchen past Midhat, who asked what was wrong. "You won't believe it," Abed said. "It takes no more than a sneeze to get that woman pregnant."

AROUND THIS TIME, Abed started to face problems at work. Bezeq was firing many of its Palestinian workers who had green West Bank IDs. Though Abed was good at his job and valued by his bosses, his position didn't feel secure. Not only was he an undesirable, the holder of a green ID, he was also, from the standpoint of a government-owned Israeli company run by a retired West

Bank commander, less than a model employee. Among his Palestinian colleagues, he always referred to Givat Shaul, the location of Bezeq's Jerusalem headquarters, as Deir Yassin, the Palestinian village on which it was built and where a notorious massacre was committed in 1948 by Zionist paramilitary forces. All of the workers under him did the same. When asked to do a job on a settler home in Sheikh Jarrah, he had refused.

The threat to Abed and the other employees with green IDs was in fact part of a larger process of cutting Palestinians off from greater Jerusalem. The Oslo Accords were purportedly for an interim period of five years that was supposed to conclude with negotiations over all the major issues, including the status of Jerusalem. In advance of those negotiations, Israel had every motivation to weaken the Palestinians' claims to the city—to diminish their presence, increase Jewish settlement, and make East Jerusalem's absorption into Israel an irrefutable fact. Building permits for Palestinians were withheld, homes were demolished, green ID holders were evicted, more checkpoints sprung up overnight, and entrance permits to the city became especially restrictive. Thousands of Palestinians who lived in the annexed parts of Jerusalem and held blue ID cards—which afforded far greater freedom of movement—had their residency revoked.

Abed's brother Nabeel was married to a woman in Dahiyat a-Salaam who had a blue ID. Because Nabeel held a green ID, he was not allowed to live in the areas annexed to Jerusalem, so the couple lived in Anata. But they had to maintain an apartment in Dahiyat a-Salaam so that Nabeel's wife could retain her Jerusalem residency and her blue ID. Periodically, Israel sent inspectors to check that she was really living there. The inspectors and their vehicles were well known in the area, so the residents would start making frantic warning calls as soon as they were spotted. When

Nabeel's wife got such a call, she would rush over to the apartment. For the crime of living with her husband just down the road, she could be cut off from the rest of her family and the city in which she had been born and raised.

Israel's process of severing Palestinians from Jerusalem meant that Abed's friend Midhat had to leave Askadinya. A Palestinian from Jordan, he didn't even have a green ID, and now he could no longer evade Israel's heightened scrutiny. He took a job as a chef at a Ramallah hotel, where he met someone with a connection to the American consul general and managed to get a visa to the United States. Midhat became a successful small business owner in the United States and never looked back.

The only Palestinians who had full access to Jerusalem and faced no threat of being kicked out were those with Israeli citizenship. They didn't have to worry about losing their residency while studying abroad or after moving in with a spouse in a neighboring town like Anata or Bethlehem. A number of men in Anata started to talk about marrying '48 Palestinians, as they were called for having remained in the part of Palestine that became Israel after 1948. Some of Abed's colleagues in Bezeq hoped this would help them keep or get back their jobs. At the time, spouses of '48 Palestinians were able to obtain permanent residency or citizenship quite easily; within two years, Israel would make it nearly impossible. Abed had a Bedouin friend who had recently married a second wife with Israeli citizenship. This friend knew many '48 Palestinian families in the north and offered to help Abed find a second wife. If the marriage didn't work out, his friend said, at least Abed would have a blue ID.

Abed mulled it over. Such a marriage could give him job security and allow him to maintain a connection to Jerusalem, no matter what new restrictions Israel might impose. He thought about a second wife mostly in utilitarian terms but admitted to himself that he was also hoping to feel less trapped.

Abed discussed it with Asmahan and her parents. As it was a way for Abed to keep his job, they raised no objections. With his Bedouin friend, he traveled to the Jaleel, the Galilee, and met the parents of several prospective brides. He told them about his children but claimed that he was divorced. The third family was from a town just north of Nazareth, Kufr Kanna, where Abed had worked in a factory for a time. The young woman's name was Jameela, meaning "beautiful." Abed thought she looked plain, but he was struck by her strong will and independence, which was a refreshing change from Asmahan. He hit it off with her parents, especially her father, and he and Jameela were engaged that same day. Not long after, her twin sister married a man with a green ID from Bethlehem.

Israeli law forbade polygamy, so in order to marry Jameela, Abed had to bring proof to the Nazareth court that he was divorced. It was just a formality, Abed told Asmahan; they would do it at the Jerusalem court on Salahadin Street and remarry there several days later, after he had gone back to Nazareth. The Jerusalem judge was on to the scheme and expressed his irritation, but the law gave him no option other than to comply.

The next step was planning a wedding celebration, without which the couple, though legally married, would be considered merely engaged. Abed now began finding reasons to delay. It was clear that Jameela loved him, and just as clear that he didn't feel the same way. When she held his hand and kissed him, they could both tell that his heart wasn't in it. The prospect of a divorce right after receiving the blue ID started to feel repugnant to him. He hadn't told the family about remarrying Asmahan, and the more time Abed spent with them, the worse he felt about the deception. Jameela's mother and father set aside a plot of land for their daughter and new son-in-law, encouraging Abed to build a house on it once he had his blue ID. They even started to buy furniture.

Abed could not see how to stay in the relationship. Telling the truth seemed out of the question, but so did continuing the lie. He kept putting off his visits to Kufr Kanna, which had become more difficult, in any case. It was the fall of 2000 and the start of the Second Intifada, which was nothing like the first—that had been a true popular uprising of general strikes, mass protests, boycotts, and acts of civil disobedience. This intifada, by contrast, had been rapidly militarized: Israel fired more than a million bullets in the first several days, after which Palestinian armed groups moved to the fore, making mass participation all but impossible.

THE IMMEDIATE TRIGGER for the uprising was the provocative visit of Ariel Sharon, champion of the settlements and ex–defense minister, to the al-Aqsa mosque compound, prompting protests. Israel responded violently, killing four unarmed Palestinians and wounding some two hundred others, many of them from Shuafat Camp and Anata. More broadly, the intifada was the culmination of years of frustration with the Oslo process, which hadn't given Palestinians freedom, independence, or an end to occupation. Nor had it put a stop to the expansion of the settlements, whose population had ballooned by more than 70 percent in the years since the first agreements were signed.

In fact, Oslo had furthered Israel's goal of holding on to maximal land with minimal Palestinians on it. The agreements had fractured the West Bank into 165 islands of limited self-government, each one surrounded by a sea of Israeli control.

Trapped in these islands and watched over by PA security forces that were subservient to Israel, Palestinians mocked the impotence of their Authority, their *sulta*, calling it a *salata*, a salad, instead. The uprising brought large numbers of IDF tanks into Palestinian cities, including the *sulta*'s administrative capital in Ramallah, where Israel laid siege to the presidential compound.

Ordinary people worried for their safety and tried to stay out of harm's way. Even '48 Palestinians felt at risk. Early in the intifada, they marched in solidarity with the occupied territories, and Israeli snipers opened fire on them. Twelve Palestinian citizens were killed, one of them a nineteen-year-old from Kufr Kanna. Hundreds attended his funeral and demonstrated against the police. Elsewhere in the Galilee, '48 Palestinians blocked roads, set tires on fire, and threw Molotov cocktails. A state commission of inquiry into these mass protests, known to Israelis as the October 2000 events, found that the deployment of sharpshooters and live fire against non-Jewish citizens had been "unjustified."

With Israel's tight restrictions on movement, it was hard for Abed to leave Anata. Before the intifada, there had been talk of him and Jameela living together in Ramallah, at least until they could be together in Kufr Kanna. Now that was unthinkable. The last place Jameela's parents wanted their daughter to live was in the West Bank. They'd heard about Israel's closures of West Bank towns, about the helicopter gunships firing missiles at buildings in Ramallah and the tanks shelling Palestinians in Beit Jala, south of Jerusalem.

They assumed Abed was coming less often because he had trouble coming into Israel, which was true but only partly. He was also trying to avoid his guilt. It had become too painful to keep up the charade with Jameela and, as time passed, harder and harder to close his eyes to their social and political differences.

Abed respected Jameela and her family, but he didn't like the way '48 Palestinians lived. Their social lives, their mannerisms, the Hebrew in their speech. They were too much like Israelis, even in a place like Kufr Kanna, which Abed considered less corrupted than other '48 Palestinian towns. One time, on their way to Tiberias, Jameela pointed out a soldier's uniform and said she thought it looked nice.

"Nice?" Abed couldn't believe his ears. "It looks *nice*? That's the uniform shooting at us in the West Bank."

"I'm sorry," she said. "I didn't mean it."

"You're a Palestinian," he told her. "You can't talk like that."

Nine months into their relationship, Jameela got into a car accident. No one told Abed. He was visiting her so infrequently that he didn't show up until more than a month after the crash. Jameela had been discharged from the hospital and was recuperating at home when she told her mother she couldn't continue with Abed. He hadn't asked after her in weeks. How could she depend on him?

At the prospect of separation, Abed felt only relief. He could stop pretending. The divorce was granted quickly: the couple had never celebrated their wedding or slept together, so their marriage was unconsummated—*zawaj bidun dukhul*, literally, marriage without entrance. Jameela's parents had no hard feelings. Her father so liked Abed that he offered to introduce him to a niece, educated and beautiful, in a nearby town. But Abed had learned his lesson. A blue ID wasn't worth breaking anyone else's heart.

VI

As the Second Intifada escalated, Abed was forced to work mostly in Jerusalem neighborhoods close to home, in Dahiyat a-Salaam and Shuafat Camp. For the time being, he still had his job at Bezeq, even without a blue ID. He was thirty-two, now the father of four daughters. One day, he was stopped in the street by Ahmad, a friend from the Democratic Front, who worked in a nearby convenience store owned by his father-in-law. Could Abed come to the father-in-law's apartment to fix a broken phone line? It was a source of distress for the extended family—there were sons in the United States who were anxiously reading the news and couldn't check in on their relatives.

Abed was acquainted with the father-in-law. He was a respected figure, the mukhtar of Dahiyat a-Salaam. Abed knew his daughters as well. They lived practically next door to Ghazl's family, and as a teenager Abed used to hand the girls letters to pass to Ghazl. The mukhtar lived just behind the convenience store, where Abed stopped to wash his hands before entering the apartment. On his way to the bathroom, Abed passed Haifa, one of the daughters who had smuggled notes to Ghazl as a child of eight or nine.

Abed said hello, but she didn't respond. Though the age difference between them was too great for Haifa to know him well, Abed was no stranger to her. A member of the DFLP, she had been at events and meetings with him.

Bothered by Haifa's snub, Abed exited the bathroom to hear Ahmad call out, "Haifa, tell your father Abed wants to come fix your phone." But once there, he couldn't find the source of the problem. He checked inside, up on the roof, and back inside the apartment again, where he eventually located the fault in the line. He passed Haifa several times and watched her with her family. She reminded him of Ghazl, and not just because she was a Hamdan. She was sharp, witty, independent minded, and politically sophisticated—everything that Asmahan was not. After Abed had fixed the line, Haifa made coffee and brought it to him and her father. Over the next few days, he found her creeping into his thoughts.

Abed called Ahmad and said he'd like to visit him at home.

"Is something wrong?" Ahmad asked.

Abed announced that he wanted to ask Haifa to be his second wife. Timidly, Ahmad said he wanted to stay out of it.

"Fine," Abed said, "but I still want to talk to Haifa's sisters."

When Abed turned up that evening, Ahmad excused himself, saying he needed to sleep. The coward! Abed thought. Haifa's sisters were in the DFLP and knew Abed well. They also knew all about his engagement to Ghazl and were even aware of his unhappiness with Asmahan. Abed slowly recounted the trouble in his marriage, explaining how he had reached this point. For seven years he had hoped Asmahan would become someone she was not, and now he wanted to change his life and marry again. He had seen Haifa the other week and hoped she would agree to be with him. Would they speak to her on his behalf?

Wafaa, Haifa's sister, promised to ask. "I hope she'll say yes," she said.

"Why 'hope'?" Abed asked. "Because you think she might refuse?"

"She's told us more than once that she's against men marrying second wives," Wafaa explained.

Abed pleaded with her to speak to Haifa anyway. "You know me. You know my family. You know my life," he said. "I don't deserve this fate. I want a chance to be happy. Please tell her that."

Ahmad called the next day, asking Abed to come over. In the living room, Wafaa said she had been reluctant to tell Haifa outright that Abed wanted to propose. Instead, she had gently broached the subject of marriage. Haifa saw right through it. Who was asking for her hand, she wanted to know.

"He's a good guy," Wafaa had said. "Well known, respected, smart, strong. Our family loves his family. There's one small reason you might object."

"What?" Haifa was impatient.

"He's married."

"As soon as I said it," Wafaa went on, "Haifa told me to leave the house. I hadn't even mentioned your name. Later, after she calmed down, she asked who it was. When I told her, she said, 'No. Not only is he married, he has daughters, too.'"

Wafaa paused. "I said you'd seen her at the store and at home, that you'd been thinking about her, that you wanted to change your life. Then Haifa began to ask questions. We sat for four hours, and at last she agreed."

"She agreed?" Abed said.

"Yes. But on one condition—you can't divorce your wife. She doesn't want to break up your family or hurt Asmahan."

Abed woke his parents early the next morning to tell them:

Haifa, the daughter of the mukhtar of Dahiyat a-Salaam, would be his second wife. She also happened to be the daughter of Abed's father's old flame, the Hamdan girl he had been prevented from marrying. Had her family agreed? his father asked. "You're married with four daughters, and you're older than her. She's beautiful, her father's a mukhtar, and her brothers work in America. Will they really accept it?"

Haifa had agreed. Abed told his father to get dressed—they were going to her parents' home. "Are you insane?" his father said. "Half the house will be asleep." Abed insisted. He was sure that all of Anata would oppose the marriage. If he let even a few hours go by, the news would spread, and Haifa and her parents might be pressured into rejecting the proposal. He could tell his mother disapproved, likely not just because of the harm it would do to Asmahan but also because she opposed men having second wives on principle. He assumed the other women in the family would be angry, too. Maybe they would refuse to speak to him. Haifa's male relatives would oppose it for their own reasons. She had cousins who wanted to marry her. Their fathers—her uncles—might try to stop the marriage. Even if they weren't against second wives, they would use it as a pretext.

Abed's father agreed to go to her family. Abed suspected that his father would have refused to do it for any woman other than his first love's daughter. When they showed up at Haifa's door, her father, Abu Awni, welcomed them. "I'm sorry for showing up so early," Abed's father said. "But this crazy son—this pushy, foolhardy son—insisted that we come now. I think you know why we're here."

"I do," Abu Awni said. "We'll consider the proposal after speaking with Haifa."

"You can speak with her now," Abed interjected.

"She's sleeping."

"You can wake her up. I know she's already agreed. You can wake her and ask her. We can't come back later."

"You're something else," Abu Awni said. He told his wife to get their daughter. Haifa was groggy coming out from her room. Abu Awni asked if she agreed to marry Abed. Haifa smiled and said yes. Abu Awni turned to Abed's father and said, "If you have a crazy son, I have a crazy daughter."

They all recited the Fatiha. Abu Awni told Abed to come back that evening to discuss the details.

"What details? Do you agree or not?" Abed asked.

"I agree," Abu Awni said.

"Does Haifa's mother agree?"

"Yes, she agrees."

"Then please go and change your clothes. We have to go to the courthouse to sign the marriage contract."

"What? Now?"

Abed knew Abu Awni would leave soon for al-Aqsa mosque—he spent all his days there—and the courthouse was on the way. "We can sign the contract before your prayers."

"Are you crazy?" Abu Awni said.

"Yes," Abed replied. "I'm crazy."

Abed's father would not come with them, forcing Abed to find a replacement witness. Two were required. He brought his brother Wa'el and a nephew working in Sheikh Jarrah. They signed the contract that morning and then Abu Awni walked to al-Aqsa.

The first person Abed wanted to tell was Naheel, and he showed up at her house later that afternoon. Naheel and Abu Wisaam could see that he was elated. He had just got engaged, he told them. Abu Wisaam's face hardened, no doubt thinking of Asmahan, his niece. Who is it? he wanted to know. It was their neighbor Haifa, Abed said, and they had already signed the contract.

"So what do you want from us?" Abu Wisaam said.

Abed needed their help. He didn't want to be alone with Asmahan when he broke the news. If Naheel and Abu Wisaam were there, Asmahan would be less likely to make a scene. Reluctantly, the two agreed. Abed went home first to retrieve his daughters and take them to his parents' place, so they wouldn't see Asmahan upset, and then he returned with Naheel and Abu Wisaam. Asmahan hadn't been expecting them and was happy to see her uncle and Naheel. It felt like a special occasion. She thought Abed had taken the girls so that the four of them could enjoy a peaceful afternoon, and she got up to make tea for her guests. While she was in the kitchen, no one said a word. Normally, Abed, Naheel, and Abu Wisaam would be joking and laughing. Asmahan had to sense that something was wrong.

She returned with glasses of sweet mint tea and sat down. Abed broke the awkward silence. He had been speaking for years about marrying again, he said. Now he had met someone, chosen someone, and had just gotten engaged.

"*Mabrouk*," congratulations, Asmahan said coldly. She started to cry and went into the bedroom, where Naheel followed her. Naheel didn't approve of Abed's decision, she said. Like Asmahan, she had only just found out. Naheel was able to coax Asmahan out of the bedroom, and she and Abed went to be with the girls while Abu Wisaam left to see his brother, Asmahan's father. Later that evening, Asmahan's father showed up, indignant and demanding to take his daughter home. Abed refused to let Asmahan go, and the argument escalated until Abed kicked her father out. Abed's father, who had been quiet during the altercation, reprimanded Abed for speaking disrespectfully to his father-in-law.

Abu Wisaam came to intervene, asking Abed to let Asmahan spend the night with her parents. Enough, he said, her father is angry. The situation is complicated. Let her go with him for two or three days to be with her family and take in the news. After that, he continued, I promise I'll bring her back. Everything will be okay.

Abed reluctantly agreed, expecting Asmahan to come home in a few days. Instead, Asmahan's parents asked Abed to give her a divorce. They wouldn't allow him to discuss it with his wife, although Abed kept pleading to see her, to speak to her on the phone. Her parents refused, saying only that they insisted on a divorce. Abed begged for Asmahan to come home to their daughters. Days and then weeks passed without contact and without Asmahan seeing her girls. After a month, Abed received a visit from Asmahan's elderly neighbor, a close friend of her parents. "Let us end this matter," he said. "Give Asmahan a divorce."

"I have a request," Abed said. "Please sit with Asmahan, alone. If she says this is what she wants, I'll meet her at the courthouse the next morning. If she wants to be with her husband and daughters, I'll bring her back to my house. But you must get her true answer, without her parents listening, and report it to me faithfully."

The neighbor did as Abed asked and confirmed it: Asmahan wanted a divorce. Abed felt that he had tried everything. If she really wished to leave, he wouldn't stop her. He had had enough of this misery. It was time to begin his new life. He told the elderly neighbor that Asmahan and her family should meet him at the Salahadin courthouse the next morning, which they did. Asmahan sat mutely, crying as her father raged against Abed. He informed the judge that his daughter rejected custody of her children, and Asmahan nodded in assent. When it was over, Abed was divorced and the sole guardian of four little girls.

HAIFA REGRETTED THAT Abed divorced Asmahan in spite of his promise not to, but she believed he had been given no choice. He had not wanted Haifa to replace Asmahan. He had hoped instead that she would complement her, fill the hole left by Ghazl's absence. Never had he thought that Haifa would become mother to his four daughters, but that is what happened. Although Asmahan continued to see the girls, Haifa embraced them as her own, and it was she who really raised them. Often Abed thought they loved her more than they loved him.

Haifa's parents also adored Abed's daughters. Her mother saw the marriage as destiny. "Look at our lives," she said to Abed. "I should have married your father, but fate wouldn't allow it. Now you've married my daughter."

Abed vowed to start anew. He would be a better husband, a better father, a better person. For the first time in his life, he started to pray. Not at the old mosque in Anata, controlled by the *sulta*, which censored any meaningful political content from the sermons of the imams, who instead bored everyone with instructions on how to wash before prayer. Abed preferred to go up the hill to the mosques of East Jerusalem—in Dahiyat a-Salaam or Shuafat Camp. There he would hear substantive political sermons, as these mosques had remained under Jordanian supervision and were comparatively free of Israel's oversight or that of the *sulta*.

After Haifa and Abed wed, Asmahan married as well, to a man from Gaza who was a security force officer in the *sulta*. This was probably how he obtained Israel's permission to relocate from Gaza to the West Bank, a move that was rarely allowed. He was quite a lot older than Asmahan and unwell, and he died about a year after they married, leaving her with an infant daughter.

At this point, Haifa wanted Abed to remarry Asmahan. Her widowhood was a sign, Haifa said. Now he could right the wrongs done to Asmahan through no fault of her own. She was sad, alone, and caring for a baby. She could use Abed's financial support.

Abed was moved by Haifa's compassion. There weren't many wives who would have made such a suggestion. He agreed to speak to Asmahan. He was sure she would say yes, not only because she was in dire straits but because she still loved him. Her parents, however, refused, and Asmahan remained alone.

HAIFA GOT PREGNANT less than a year after the wedding. Her doctor was in Jerusalem, on the other side of the checkpoint. At the time, all Palestinians in Anata and Jerusalem were eligible to use the city's hospitals without a permit. Though it was a hassle to get through the checkpoint, most pregnant women still chose to go to Jerusalem, less because the care was better than that they wanted to secure the next generation's ties to the capital, the heart of the Palestinian homeland. When Haifa went into labor several weeks early, Abed brought her and her parents in a shared taxi to the main checkpoint at Shuafat Camp. The Border Police saw that she was in labor but refused to let her through. Abed told the driver to try a second checkpoint at the other end of the refugee camp, in Ras Khamis.

There Abed approached a pair of Border Police, a woman and a man. They also could see that Haifa was in labor. The woman officer asked for cigarettes, and when Abed handed her two, one for her and one for her colleague, she agreed to let them pass. The checkpoint road had large cement blocks preventing cars from crossing. Haifa had to get out of the taxi with her parents and shuffle to a cab on the other side. Abed was in his work clothes and he wasn't carrying his green ID. He told the guard that Haifa and her parents would continue on to the Red Crescent Hospital in a-Suwana, just east of the Old City walls, while he would go home, shower, pick up his ID, and take another taxi back. She agreed to let him through when he returned.

Soon after, Abed reached the checkpoint again and reminded the officer of her pledge. She asked for two more cigarettes and let him cross. By the time Abed got to the maternity ward, Haifa had given birth to their son. They decided to call him Adam, father of humankind. Three years later, Haifa delivered a second boy, this time at Makassed Hospital on the Mount of Olives. He was smaller and more delicate than Adam. They named him "birth," Milad.

PART TWO

Two Fires

_____

VII

On the morning of the accident, Huda Dahbour left her Ramallah apartment and struggled through the wind and rain to meet her staff at Clock Tower Square. A fifty-one-year-old endocrinologist and single mother, she managed a mobile health clinic run by UNRWA, the UN organization for Palestinian refugees. She had been at the job for sixteen years, working at UNRWA's Jerusalem headquarters in Sheikh Jarrah until Israel made it impossible for her to enter the city. Now she treated patients in a mobile clinic in the West Bank.

Three members of her medical team joined her at Clock Tower Square. They were scheduled to make their regular visit to the Bedouin encampment of Khan al-Ahmar. Getting into the minibus, they greeted their driver, Abu Faraj, a Bedouin man with white hair and a white mustache. In addition to driving, he served as a sort of cultural advisor, helping Huda and her team navigate local rivalries and tribal customs.

Khan al-Ahmar was home to Bedouin of the Jahalin tribe who had been expelled from the Naqab in the years after the founding of Israel. Most of the tens of thousands of Naqab Bedouin had been forcibly displaced in 1948, fleeing to the West Bank, Gaza, and neighboring countries. In the four years following the war, Israel expelled some seventeen thousand more. In total, around 85 percent of the population was removed. Those who remained in the Naqab were corralled into a reservation, the *siyaaj*, or fence, while their land was confiscated. Along with the majority of Israel's Palestinian citizens, they lived for eighteen years under the rule of a military government, which imposed curfews, travel restrictions, a ban on political parties, detention without trial, and closed security zones.

Forced at gunpoint to leave the Naqab and cross into the West Bank, the Jahalin Bedouin made their way north to the desert hills outside Jerusalem. There they were expelled once again to make room for the settlement of Ma'ale Adumim. When they reached nearby Khan al-Ahmar, they requested permission to stay there from the land's owner, Abed's grandfather. He initially rebuffed them. Abed's family, like many in Anata, distrusted the local Bedouin. Some of them encroached on other people's property, took handouts of UN food and made a business of reselling it, and ignored bills for municipal services, claiming that their Bedouin practices did not recognize bourgeois activities like paying taxes.

They squatted on Khan al-Ahmar anyway. Eventually, Abed's grandfather came to see the value of their presence on his land: since he wasn't allowed to access it himself, having the Bedouin there made Israeli expropriation more difficult. Settlers considered the encampment an eyesore, and Israeli planners wanted the area cleared of Palestinians. When Israel issued demolition orders for the rusted tin shanties and schoolhouse made of car tires, Abed's family provided documents showing that the Bedouin had been given permission to live on the Salamas' land.

Huda did what she could for the impoverished Bedouin. Though forbidden to treat their goats or take them in UN vehicles to buy provisions, she did so regardless. At the UN, she was known for flouting the rules when her conscience dictated it. Despite repeated warnings from her bosses against engaging in political activity, Huda brought her staff to protest Israeli attacks on Gaza, and on one occasion she took them to give flowers to women political prisoners being released from Israeli jails. After UNRWA made cost-cutting changes that limited prenatal treatment to patients considered at risk, Huda gave the designation to every pregnant woman she encountered. Confronted by her supervisor, she proudly admitted her transgression and vowed to carry on doing it until the regulations were changed.

LEAVING CLOCK TOWER Square, Abu Faraj called the sheikh of Khan al-Ahmar to confirm that Huda and her team were on their way. The villagers had prepared a ceremonial welcome tent to greet them before the UN staff treated the women, children, and men. Heading south, the team sang along, as they always did, to Fairuz, Huda's favorite singer. After they stopped to pick up the data entry clerk at the Qalandia refugee camp, the pharmacist, Nidaa, said she felt nauseated. Huda thought she looked pale. A young mother of two small children, Nidaa was several months pregnant with a third. Huda told Abu Faraj to pull over so they could get her some food. They turned off at a roundabout and entered a-Ram, an urban area facing the settlement of Neve Yaakov and surrounded on three sides by the separation wall. It was cold, wet, and dreary. They drank tea and ate *ka'ek* with zaatar and falafel. Now running late for Khan al-Ahmar, they exited a-Ram for the Jaba road and came face-to-face with a horrific sight: a school bus flipped on its side, its doors against the ground, its front engulfed in flames.

The Jaba road was originally built to take settlers to and from Jerusalem without having to enter Ramallah. It was one of many such bypass roads, designed to reduce commute times for the settlers, give them a sense of safety, and create the illusion of a continuous Jewish presence from the city to the settlements. After Israel built new bypass roads, this one came to be used mostly by Palestinians.

It had been carved through an escarpment, forming a deep chasm with tall rocky cliffs on both sides. The village of Jaba perched atop one cliff; a-Ram was on the other. The road had two lanes heading toward the Qalandia checkpoint, and one going in the opposite direction, toward the Jaba checkpoint, and there was no center divider. The single eastern lane served as the main route around blocked-off Jerusalem for some 200,000 people, but the Jaba checkpoint was not permanently staffed. Soldiers were there to stop cars mostly during the morning and evening commutes to reduce the flow of Palestinian traffic onto a road shared with settlers. So at rush hour, the Jaba road was clogged with a long line of Palestinian buses, trucks, and cars. As drivers neared the bottleneck, only minutes after having escaped the maddening gridlock at Qalandia, some would overtake slow-moving vehicles by veering into a lane of opposing traffic. This had caused so many accidents that the artery came to be called "the death road."

Huda asked Abu Faraj to pull over. People were exiting their cars and converging around the overturned school bus. Because the road was wet and oily, Abu Faraj stopped the van sideways to prevent oncoming cars from sliding into the gathering crowd. Huda and her team jumped out and rushed to the front of the bus. Behind it they could see an eighteen-wheel trailer truck that had come to a diagonal halt across two of the road's three lanes.

Salem, one of the onlookers, lived just a few hundred feet away but he spoke in the heavily accented drawl of a Hebronite. He had kept his children home that morning because of the pelting rain and heavy fog. In all his thirty-eight years, he had never seen rain like that. He was on his way to work when he saw the overturned bus, stopped his car in the middle of the road, and ran toward it.

Huda called to Salem and a few other men nearby to get the driver out, since he was close to the fire. As they began to pull at him, he yelled to them to save the children and their teachers. Until that moment, Huda hadn't realized there were children on the bus. Her colleagues would remember the children screaming, but Huda either erased the memory or blocked out the sound. Together with Salem, they yanked at the driver, whose body was stuck and his legs aflame. When they finally managed to free him, the rain doused the fire on his legs.

They laid him at the side of the road, the smoke still rising from his knees, and rushed back to the front of the bus to reach for a teacher, who had been sitting behind him. While they were grabbing her, she shouted that they should leave her and save the children. At this, Nidaa began to convulse and shriek. Huda hurried her back to the UNRWA van and told her not to get out.

Abu Faraj, in the meantime, was directing traffic, keeping a path clear for the eventual evacuation of the wounded. He now ran past the burning bus and splayed semitrailer to the Jaba checkpoint a few hundred feet down the road, thinking to beg the soldiers there to help with the rescue. The smoke was visible at the checkpoint, but the soldiers, who seemed frightened, shouted at him to stay back and not come any closer.

At this point, the fire was too fierce to continue pulling any-one out from the front of the bus. But it had not yet reached the back, where, as far as Huda could see, most of the children were crammed. Salem wanted to break the rear windows to get the children out. Huda wasn't sure it was a good idea. No one had a better one, though, and there seemed to be no soldiers, police, fire trucks, or ambulances on the way, despite people in the crowd who kept frantically phoning the Israeli and Palestin-ian emergency services. One of Huda's team even called a relative who worked in the Palestinian parliament.

Huda and the others close to the bus agreed that Salem should smash the rear windows using a small fire extinguisher, which one of the bystanders had brought from his car. The moment the back window shattered, Huda heard a whoosh of oxygen and saw the flames around the bus shoot up into the air. The fire now doubled in height, sending up thick, black plumes of smoke that rose above the cliff.

Huda watched in shock as Salem crawled into the burning bus. He could hear the kindergartners crying and screaming. Some of them tried to climb up on the overturned seats and jump to the windows above them. Two teachers managed to escape through the smashed windows and brought several of the children out with them.

Ula Joulani, one of the teachers, was on the trip with her nephew Saadi, who was in her kindergarten class. She was like a second mother to Saadi. That morning, as on every weekday, Ula had driven to her parents' home, where Saadi and his family lived. Complaining about the terrible weather, her mother didn't think Saadi should go on the trip. Ula laughed, asking her mother if she wanted a refund. Ula had paid the fee for one of her students, an orphan, and had promised to take care of another child, the son of a friend, who, like Saadi's grandmother, had reservations about the outing.

After Ula made it out of the burning bus, she heard the trapped children calling her name. So she followed Salem back inside, the only other person to do so. Salem, hunched in the bus, had managed to open some of the side windows. He and Ula lifted the children up and through the back of the bus as Huda and the others formed a line, handing the kindergartners down one by one. High above the road, at the top of the cliffs, dozens of villagers had gathered from Jaba and a-Ram. Some of the Jaba Bedouin brought large tanks of water that they poured onto the flames and through the open bus windows, helping to keep Salem and Ula from burning. At the side of the bus, the crowd tried to hose them down using small fire extinguishers.

Ula and Salem managed to rescue dozens of the children. As they progressed toward the front of the bus, where the flames were strongest, the children they reached were in worse and worse shape. Some were charred from head to toe. They were placed on the road face up, their knees bent up to their chests. Had he not known otherwise, Salem would not have recognized them as human. One girl, who was blackened all over, had been set on the ground with the dead children when a nurse working with Huda saw that she was still breathing. Huda and the nurse lifted her up and put her in the backseat of a car that would take her to the hospital.

The stench of burned hair and flesh was overpowering. Huda had read somewhere that smell was the sense most strongly linked to memory. Perhaps that was why, standing there amid the carnage, she was taken back to the worst day of her life.

Palestine and Israel

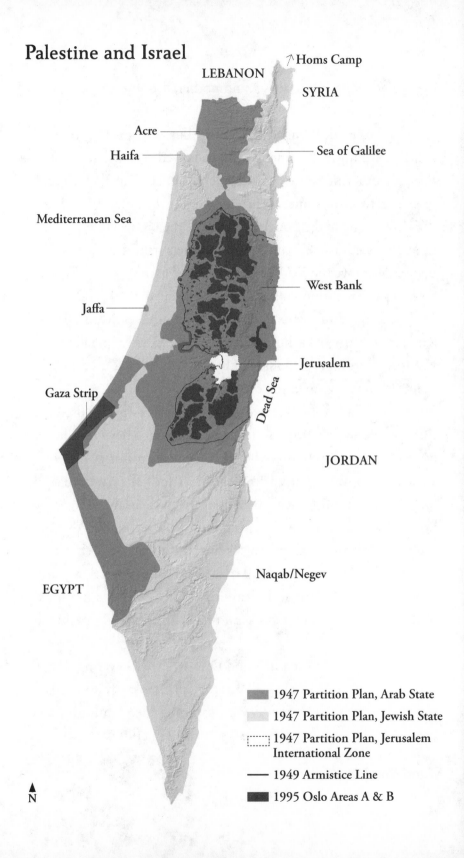

Homs Camp

LEBANON

SYRIA

Acre

Haifa

Sea of Galilee

Mediterranean Sea

West Bank

Jaffa

Jerusalem

Gaza Strip

Dead Sea

JORDAN

Naqab/Negev

EGYPT

N

■ 1947 Partition Plan, Arab State

  1947 Partition Plan, Jewish State

⌐⌐ 1947 Partition Plan, Jerusalem
     International Zone

— 1949 Armistice Line

■ 1995 Oslo Areas A & B

VIII

In the summer of 1985, Huda was a twenty-five-year-old doctor fresh out of medical school at Damascus University. Her father suggested that she join the Palestine Red Crescent in Tunisia, where her uncle, who was a senior official in the PLO, would be able to look after her. The PLO's headquarters were based in Tunis, having moved there after Israel had forced the organization out of Lebanon. Although Huda's father supported Fatah, he did not consider himself very political. He told Huda he thought both the left and the right were too uncompromising. Huda attributed his moderation to his childhood in Haifa, with its Muslim, Christian, and Jewish populations living side by side.

Huda had grown up on stories of Haifa. The Dahbours came from Wadi Nisnas, a neighborhood between the port and the terraced gardens of the Baha'i shrine on the slope of Mount Carmel. On the Sabbath, when Jews are forbidden from performing various everyday tasks, Huda's family would go to their Jewish neighbors to turn on the lights or the heat.

Huda's grandmother was born in Ottoman Haifa during World War I. A noted beauty, she married her cousin as arranged by her family, giving birth to her first child, Huda's father, Mustafa, at seventeen. Mustafa was almost fourteen years old when the UN voted to partition Palestine in November 1947. The decision triggered a civil war that culminated in the Nakba, the mass expulsion and flight of more than 80 percent of Palestinians from the territory that became Israel.

In April 1948, several months into the civil war and just days before Passover, the British Mandatory forces governing the country began to withdraw from Haifa. As the British departed, Jewish paramilitary units launched an attack on the Palestinian parts of the city, calling it Operation Bi'ur Chametz, a reference to the ritual purging of bread from Jewish homes before the start of Passover. From the hillside Jewish neighborhoods, they shelled the Palestinian homes and downtown markets below. Haifa fell in a day.

Through Arabic radio broadcasts and vans equipped with loudspeakers, the Jewish forces blared instructions to evacuate immediately. The conquering battalion had been ordered to firebomb "all objectives that can be set alight" and "kill every Arab encountered." Barrels stuffed with kerosene-soaked rags and fitted with ignition devices were sent hurtling downhill into the Palestinian areas. The Jews "were continually shooting down on all Arabs who moved both in Wadi Nisnas and the Old City," a British intelligence officer reported. "This included completely indiscriminate and revolting machinegun fire, mortar fire and sniping on women and children sheltering in churches and attempting to get out." Much of the city was ethnically cleansed by the time Passover began. The smoke-filled streets downtown were buried under bodies and rubble as families fled the advancing columns. Terrified survivors rushed to the port, trampling each other in the stampede. Empty Palestinian homes were quickly given to new Jewish immigrants to ensure that the original owners could not return.

Huda's family fled on a convoy of trucks heading north to Lebanon. Her grandmother talked of their terror, fueled by stories of rapes and massacres. That the Jewish neighbors promised to look after their house gave them little comfort. Three weeks after the fall of Haifa, Israel declared independence. By that time, some quarter of a million Palestinians had been made refugees, among them 90 percent of the Arab residents of Haifa and Jaffa, the most populous Palestinian cities. Israel's war with the neighboring Arab states had not yet begun.

After days of travel, the Dahbours were destitute and hungry. On their way north, while still in Palestine, Huda's grandmother entered a cave and gave birth to a girl. They cut the umbilical cord with a cleaning pin from a paraffin stove. The makeshift delivery inspired them to name her Maryam, for the Virgin Mary. Parceling out their last crumbs of bread, they reached the Lebanese coastal city of Sidon, and from there they went to Homs, in Syria. The refugees were gathered in the medieval citadel, then taken to the stables of a military barracks built during the French mandate. There UNRWA established what would become known as Homs Camp.

Because families from the same Palestinian villages and cities lived together in the camp, the different areas were named after the refugees' hometowns. Haifa was at the camp entrance, reflecting its importance. Most of the other refugees were from the Galilee, though some were from Acre and Jaffa. The streets were also named after Palestinian towns, from Hebron and Jerusalem to Nazareth, Safed, and Tarshiha. There was no water or electricity and little insulation, and everyone used communal outhouses. UNRWA distributed sacks of used clothes, often with mismatched shoes. One year at the end of Ramadan, on Eid al-Fitr, Huda's grandmother had the idea of dyeing the used children's clothes in blue ink so that they would have presents for Eid that looked new. Practically every woman followed suit, turning the camp into a sea of blue. In wintertime, the rain banged loudly on the corrugated zinc roof and it was hard to breathe through the smog of the paraffin stove.

Yet despite the poverty, the separation from family, and the bitterness of exile, the Dahbours managed to find happiness. When Huda's father married, the family hung blankets in their one room to give him and his bride some privacy. Afterward, he set about improving their accommodations, building an indoor bathroom and digging a well in the courtyard. Their door was always open, and Mustafa allowed the entire camp to make use of the fresh, clear well water.

With no electricity in the camp, the family spent their evenings listening to stories, and in particular those told by Huda's grandmother. She raised Huda and her siblings, cousins, aunts, and uncles on tales of a magical place called Haifa, where the Carmel mountain moved when children played on it and the raindrops never touched people's heads. Haifa was paradise. Huda and her siblings went to sleep dreaming of this mythic Haifa. When they cried that they wanted to see Haifa, the adults filled large barrels with water and put the children in to splash about, telling them to close their eyes and imagine they were in the Haifa sea.

Most of the boys and men in Homs Camp, including Huda's father, had initially joined pan-Arab nationalist movements but switched their allegiance to Fatah as it grew in strength in the 1960s. Huda's youngest uncle, Kamel, was the only one of his generation born outside Palestine. He was just four years older than Huda and looked different from his siblings, with browner skin, darker eyes, and a serious countenance. He was the first in the family to join Fatah. As an adolescent he listened to their songs and later trained with them in the camp. At fifteen, he left Homs to enlist with Fatah in Lebanon. Kamel came back to visit the family every few months. They were overjoyed to see him, but he had strict conditions: they had to act as if he had never been away—no tears and no hugs, otherwise he would leave and not return. When he came through the door, Huda and her grandmother had to restrain themselves from leaping up to embrace him. After a week, he would disappear again without saying goodbye.

Huda's grandmother would sit on the ground and weep. She worried that her youngest boy would die with Fatah. In Syria, the male Palestinian refugees were required to perform compulsory military service. They were recruited into the Palestine Liberation Army, officially the military wing of the PLO but in fact controlled by the Syrian army. During one of Kamel's visits home, Huda's grandmother reported his arrival to the authorities, who took him to serve in the PLA. He was bitterly opposed to being part of the Syrian army, which soon turned its guns on Fatah in the Lebanese Civil War. Huda's grandmother thought it was the only way to keep him safe, but she and Huda cried as he was taken away against his will.

Kamel deserted the PLA when Syria backed the Lebanese Christian militias that had laid siege to a Palestinian refugee camp, Tel al-Zaatar. He rejoined his comrades in Fatah who were defending the camp. The siege lasted fifty-two days, and when the camp fell, the Christian militias massacred thousands of Palestinians. Huda's family got word that Kamel had been at Tel al-Zaatar, but they heard nothing more. They searched for information until at last they obtained the bloodied shirt he had worn on the day he died. Huda's grandmother clung to the shirt in her grief. She never recovered from Kamel's death, blaming herself for having reported him to the Syrian authorities. If not for that, he might never have been in Tel al-Zaatar.

The keeper of the family's memories was Huda's uncle Ahmad, who had left Palestine on his second birthday. He, too, had grown up on his mother's stories of Haifa, of the bakery they had owned and of their neighbors. Nurtured on this history, he became a renowned Palestinian poet, publishing his first book at eighteen. His poems told the story of his scattered family, his grieving mother and her tales of Haifa, his little brother killed in Tel al-Zaatar, his family's poverty in the refugee camp. Millions of children recited his words in school, and his poems, put to music, came to be some of the most popular songs of the Palestinian revolution. Known as the Lover of Haifa, Ahmad was eventually appointed general director of the PLO's Culture Department.

After graduating from medical school, Huda agreed to join her uncle Ahmad in Tunis. The PLO was then at one of the weakest points in its history. It had lost its territorial base in Lebanon, with its fighters now scattered across the Arab world, most of them far from the territory they sought to liberate. The organization was internally riven, and there were calls to overthrow its leader, Yasser Arafat. Jordan and Israel were cooperating in the occupied territories, Syria supported PLO dissident factions, and the strongest Arab military power, Egypt, had formed a separate peace with Israel.

In September 1985, Israel captured a top Fatah commander and three senior officers as they sailed from Cyprus to Lebanon, severely torturing the commander. In retaliation, a Fatah squad captured an Israeli yacht in Cyprus, demanding the release of their colleagues and killing the Israelis on board. This occurred on Yom Kippur, the day of atonement. Israel responded six days later, on October 1.

The PLO's headquarters were in Hammam Chott, a coastline suburb of Tunis. Due to meet that morning were the organization's most senior leaders, among them Yasser Arafat and his deputies Abu Jihad and Abu Iyad and dozens of others, including Ahmad Dahbour. Soon after the scheduled start, eight Israeli F-15s flew overhead and dropped 500- and 2,000-pound bombs, leaving the complex in ruins. More than sixty Palestinians and Tunisians were killed.

At the time, Huda was stationed sixty miles away with the Palestine Red Crescent at Medjez el-Bab, where she treated the families of PLO fighters. On the morning of October 1, she was told to evacuate the staff and patients immediately: after the attack on Hammam Chott, there was fear that Medjez el-Bab might be next.

Huda rushed to Hammam Chott, scared that her uncle had been killed. When she got there, an hour and a half after the assault, she confronted a hellscape of wreckage, ash, and bodies. It looked to her like the end of the world. Muddy water filled a giant crater where one of the buildings had stood. Bulldozers were already there, clearing debris of smashed concrete, twisted beams, and shards of metal. Doctors and nurses, coated in a thick layer of gray dust, dug in the rubble for the dead and injured. Teams of rescue workers carried limp bodies on stretchers. Ambulance sirens screamed over the cries of the wounded. Friends and family searched through the detritus, shouting out names of the missing. The putrid smell of death was everywhere.

Though she was just twenty-five, Huda had seen her share of horrors. She had lived through the wars in 1967 and 1973, when Israeli bombs had blown up the oil refinery in Homs. As a medical student in 1982, she had tended to the wounded Palestinians evacuated from Lebanon. But Hammam Chott was incomparably worse. Huda expected to treat the injured, but her boss ordered her to retrieve body parts instead. All around she heard sobbing and wailing, sounds that would remain with her for days. She vomited as she did her work.

Afterward, she was sent on a job no less awful, visiting the families of the dead. She was a young doctor with no experience, and the only female physician present. She entered the homes of mothers, fathers, and children who were howling in grief. She prescribed Valium for them to calm their nerves. The face of one bereft young woman, a newlywed who had lost her groom, haunted Huda's nights.

Israel had come close to taking out much of the Palestinian national movement in a single blow. But the meeting had been postponed at the last minute, and most of the senior leaders were either not there or as usual were running late. Arafat and his deputies survived, as did Huda's uncle. The underlings who had showed up on time were killed.

The bombing had shocked Huda's family, who had been trying to find her throughout the day after hearing that a woman with the same name had died in the attack. They were not the only ones in shock. Huda noticed a change in the survivors, including Arafat and the other top PLO figures. She suspected that the near-death experience, and the realization that Israel could have eliminated the whole organization, accelerated their move toward accommodation. Three years later, in 1988, the PLO offered Israel a historic compromise, consenting to a Palestinian state in the occupied territories, just 22 percent of the homeland. The proposed state excluded Haifa, Jaffa, and the other towns its leaders had been exiled from, the places to which they had spent decades fighting to return.

IX

Huda met her husband, Ismail, shortly after the attack on Hammam Chott. He had come to her clinic with tonsillitis while on a visit from Moscow, where he was completing his doctorate in international relations. He was also the head of the Palestinian student union there, a fast track to national political leadership, and was in Tunis for a meeting of student union activists from around the world. Five years older than Huda, Ismail looked a bit like the hero in an action movie, with a mane of shaggy, sandy brown hair and a thick mustache. Huda had three conditions for any potential mate: he had to be educated, a member of Fatah—which to her meant a person of moderation, like her father—and, unlike most of the men she knew, not intimidated by a successful, intelligent woman. In concrete terms, that involved supporting her plan to resume medical school to become a specialist. Ismail met all three.

They were engaged five days after they met and then Ismail returned to Moscow. Huda joined him the following year, living in the university dorms. She loved Moscow and Russian culture, impressed with how literate and well educated the people were. After learning Russian, she began studying pediatrics but soon got pregnant, and it changed her in ways she hadn't expected. She could no longer bear the sight and sound of children in pain. Huda was ready to switch fields when Ismail learned that Arafat had appointed him to a diplomatic posting in Bucharest. She talked to one of her teachers about staying alone in Moscow to complete her training. The teacher advised against it: husband and wife are like a needle and thread—where the needle goes, the thread must follow.

In Bucharest, Huda had to start again, learning Romanian and applying to a new medical school. She took it as an opportunity to change her specialty to endocrinology. She enjoyed the logic and critical reasoning that the profession entailed and, more practically, thought there would be no emergency work, so that after her child was born she would not have to be away at night.

They named their baby daughter Hiba, "gift." The birth put a strain on the marriage. Hiba was difficult, crying without end, and Huda received little support or sympathy from Ismail. She was single-handedly nursing and taking care of Hiba, studying endocrinology, serving food to poor Palestinian students in Romania, and hosting dinner parties for diplomats, visiting Palestinians, and Romanian officials. A few months after Hiba's birth, she became pregnant again. By the end of her third trimester, she was worn out from a year of soothing Hiba's relentless crying, so she chose an aspirational name for the second baby, a boy—Hadi, meaning "calm." She traveled to give birth to Hadi in Homs, where she had the support of family. Back at home, Ismail maintained that the stress was of her own making: she was the one who chose to stay in medical school while raising two young children who were just a year apart. If she wanted to pursue her specialty, he had no objection. But he would not be helping with cooking, childcare, or hosting; she was free to study when all of that was done.

Somehow she managed, learning Romanian, finishing her training, raising her children, hosting dinners, and even having a third child, Ahmad, in 1991. Though exhausted and unhappy in her marriage, she appeared to be fortunate and content: a successful doctor with a distinguished husband and three young children.

After the Oslo Accords, thousands of PLO cadres were able to return to the newly formed pockets of Palestinian autonomy in Gaza and the West Bank. Though Huda wasn't eligible to go on her own, not having worked for the PLO, she could do so with Ismail. But he didn't want to leave Bucharest, a riverside capital dubbed the Paris of the East. He enjoyed the life of a diplomat. Huda insisted on leaving, however. She knew Israel, she said: if they didn't go now, they would not be allowed to enter Palestine later. Privately, she had another reason for wanting to go. Despite the state of her marriage and her husband's refusal to help, she dreamed of having a child born on Palestinian soil. This was her chance to replant a seed in the land from which her family had been uprooted.

They arrived in September 1995, a year before Israel halted entry of PLO personnel. Huda gave birth to their fourth child the following year, naming the girl Lujain, which meant "silver" and came from the opening line of one of her favorite Fairuz songs. It was the peak of what was called the peace process. Prime Minister Yitzhak Rabin had just concluded the second Oslo Accord, known as Oslo II, which delineated all the islands of limited Palestinian autonomy in the occupied territories. Huda felt it was meaningless.

Rabin was emphatic that there would be no Palestinian state, no capital in Jerusalem, more settlements annexed to Jerusalem, more settlement blocs in the West Bank, and that Israel would never return to the boundaries it had prior to the 1967 war, even though they comprised a full 78 percent of historic Palestine. Somewhere within the West Bank and Gaza, the remaining 22 percent—or the part of it that Israel hadn't settled, annexed, or set aside for permanent military control—the Palestinians would be granted "less than a state," as Rabin called it. But even these crumbs were too much for some Israelis: Rabin was assassinated by an Orthodox Jewish nationalist a little over a month after Huda and Ismail and their children crossed into the West Bank. Hearing the news at his home in Gaza, Yasser Arafat wept.

The Palestinians who came to the occupied territories under Oslo were known as returnees. Huda thought the term was silly. She was a refugee in Syria, an expatriate when briefly living with her parents in the Gulf, an immigrant in Romania, and now a returnee. She was on Palestinian land, but to what had she returned? Not to anyplace she or her father or uncle or grandmother knew. Huda's husband was not allowed to return to his family's home in Jabal Mukaber, because it was within annexed Jerusalem. He and Huda moved instead to part of neighboring Sawahre, just outside the municipal boundary. Sawahre and Jabal Mukaber had once been a single village but, after Oslo, Palestinians from eastern Sawahre needed permits to visit their relatives in Jabal Mukaber and even to bury their dead in the cemetery. Later the separation wall ran through the middle of Sawahre.

Huda felt out of place there. The villagers seemed rough-mannered to her, as though out of another time. Their dialect was hard for her to understand, and she was embarrassed not to comprehend the basic speech of fellow Palestinians. Her neighbors struck her as hardened, too. They were mountain people, nothing like the cosmopolitan, seaside Haifa natives of her grandmother's stories. Even Haifa itself, when she was finally able to visit, bore no resemblance to her grandmother's descriptions.

As a returnee, Huda felt a growing distance from the society around her. The returnees who had come with Arafat filled the senior positions in the new *sulta* at the expense of the local Palestinians who had led the intifada. It was only due to the sacrifice of the local population, the "insiders," that the outsiders were able to return. But the lives of the insiders only got worse after Oslo. On top of greater restrictions on movement, employment plummeted as Israel replaced Palestinian laborers with foreign workers, recruited mostly from Asia. The year after Huda arrived, almost one in three Palestinians was out of work. Nearly every returnee, by contrast, had a job in Arafat's expanding patronage network.

Ordinary people came to resent the returnees, holding them responsible for Oslo, corruption, and the impossible bind of the Palestinian security forces, which were key to maintaining Israel's occupation. The figures close to Arafat pocketed tens of millions of dollars of public money, much of it funneled through a Tel Aviv bank account, and some even profited from the building of settlements. Arafat tried to make light of the matter. He once told his cabinet he had just received a call from his wife reporting a thief in the house; he assured her it was impossible because all the thieves were sitting right there with him.

Joking aside, Arafat knew he was threatened by the widespread unhappiness with Oslo—and with the authoritarian regime it had created. When twenty prominent figures signed a petition against the *sulta*'s "corruption, deceit and despotism," more than half of them were detained, interrogated, or placed under house arrest. Others were beaten or shot in the legs.

Huda was most troubled by the *sulta*'s security cooperation with Israel. Ismail worked in the Interior Ministry, which, relying on a wide network of informants, oversaw the surveillance and arrest of Palestinians who continued to resist Israel's occupation. Huda was horrified by how many Palestinians were betraying one another. Even among her own staff at the UNRWA clinic, there were informants who brought on visits and interrogation by Israeli intelligence. Huda refused to change her behavior or censor herself, however, remaining defiantly political at work. For her, the job was never only humanitarian. It was always national, too. Treating refugees meant she was doing something for her people.

X

Jerusalem was still relatively open when Huda first arrived in Sawahre. She was able to send her children to school in the city. Below the age of twelve, they didn't need a blue ID to enter. But over time the restrictions grew, and from one day to the next Jerusalem was closed off. On one occasion, the school buses had no way to bring the students home to Sawahre. Huda and half the parents of the village spent the afternoon searching for their children, who finally showed up at sunset, after walking for several hours. Huda immediately took them out of their Jerusalem schools.

It was a fateful decision. Until then, Hadi had lived up to his name. He was a quiet boy who rarely got into trouble. That changed when he was sent to a new school in Abu Dis, which was home to al-Quds University and the site of frequent clashes with Israeli soldiers. During the Second Intifada, in late 2003, Israel erected the separation wall through Abu Dis, causing merchants, whose income relied heavily on customers from Jerusalem, to lose business. Shops closed, land values dropped by more than half, rental prices by nearly a third, and those who could afford to moved away.

Israeli troops were stationed outside Hadi's school practically every day. To Huda, their presence seemed designed to provoke the students so as to arrest as many of them as possible. The soldiers would stop them on their way out of classes, line them up against the wall, frisk them, and sometimes beat them, too.

In her work at the UNRWA camps around the West Bank, Huda saw things that made her afraid for her sons. She had witnessed a soldier shoot a boy who threw a stone at a tank. The soldiers stopped her from going to help him as he fell to the ground. At home in Sawahre, listening to the nightly news of West Bank killings and closures, she had trouble sleeping. She knew Hadi was out throwing stones.

The stress began to show in her body. It started with headaches that became severe. Then at work one day she had the sensation of cold liquid inside her head. She had double vision and difficulty walking. Back home in Sawahre, she took a nap, waking up twenty-four hours later. Huda understood that she had been in a coma, a sign that she might have a cerebral hemorrhage. The Palestinian hospitals in the West Bank and East Jerusalem weren't equipped to perform the operation, she was told. She couldn't afford treatment in Israel. Finally she obtained a letter from Arafat promising to cover 90 percent of the 50,000 shekels in costs and brought it to Hadassah Hospital in Jerusalem.

The surgery was a success, but the stress that had possibly caused the hemorrhage only intensified. One Sunday in May 2004, when Hadi was fifteen and a half, he and his friends were shot at by Israeli Border Police, a gendarmerie that operated under the command of the army when in Abu Dis and of the police when in annexed East Jerusalem. Eyewitnesses told the

Israeli human rights group B'Tselem and the AFP news agency
that the boys had not taken part in any hostilities. Hadi told his
mother that they had been minding their own business, drinking
Cokes, when the soldiers started to fire at them as if in a sort of
game. One of the bullets hit Hadi's friend, who was sitting right
beside him. The boy was killed immediately.

After that, Hadi confronted the soldiers with new determination.
Huda would see him and his friends in the street, recognizing him
despite the black-and-white kaffiyeh covering his face. She kept
her distance, though, not wanting the soldiers to see she was his
mother and then come to their home to arrest him at night. But
her efforts failed to protect him. Less than a year after Hadi's friend
was shot, Israeli jeeps and armored vehicles surrounded Huda's
home. Troops approached from all sides and banged loudly on the
door. Huda knew why they had come.

Hadi was sixteen. Huda wanted to delay the inevitable, to
have a few more seconds with her boy, so she ignored the banging,
opening the door only when the soldiers began kicking at it. They
had their weapons trained on her as she asked what they wanted,
tears silently running down her face.

"We want Hadi," one of the soldiers said. Huda demanded to
know the accusation. "Your son knows," she was told.

"I'm his mother. I want to know." They ignored her.

Thirteen-year-old Ahmad came with her as she led the way to
Hadi's room. Ahmad told his mother not to cry; it would only
make it harder for Hadi. Huda tried to contain her fear, knowing
that any attempt to stop the soldiers from taking Hadi could put
his life in danger. She imagined them killing him there in front of
her, saying that it was in self-defense. Huda wanted to hug Hadi,
but if she touched him she would fall apart. She asked the soldiers
to let him take a winter coat. It was still cold. Where would she be

able to find him, she wanted to know; she was told to come see him in the morning in the nearby settlement of Ma'ale Adumim. She watched them put zip ties around his wrists, pushing him out the door and through the garden toward one of the jeeps. It felt as if her heart had left with him.

For two weeks, Huda drove from one detention facility to another in search of Hadi, from Ma'ale Adumim to Ofer prison to Moscobiya in Jerusalem to Gush Etzion, using her UNWRA work permit to pass checkpoints and enter settlements barred to green ID holders. But she never saw Hadi and was unable to learn where he was being held. She couldn't eat, couldn't sleep, couldn't laugh, couldn't smile. She couldn't bring herself to prepare any of the dishes that Hadi liked. She didn't want to leave her house or go anywhere she might be forced to carry on a normal conversation, as if she weren't in the deepest grief, as if Hadi were not gone.

Huda retained a Palestinian lawyer with a blue ID who charged $3,000. Ismail refused to pay. He blamed Hadi and Huda for the arrest. Why had Hadi been out throwing stones and not at school? Why hadn't she stopped him? For Huda, this was more than she could bear. If Ismail was unwilling to act as a father, she no longer wanted him in her life. Quoting a passage from the Quran in which Khader, a servant of God, parts with Moses, she asked for a divorce. If you refuse to grant it, she said, I will tell everyone that you're not a nationalist and you won't support your son. Huda saw that she had frightened him, and Ismail agreed to give her the divorce.

After two weeks, the lawyer called to say that Hadi was being held at a detention center in the Gush Etzion settlement bloc, south of Bethlehem, and would soon have a hearing at the military court at the Ofer prison, between Jerusalem and Ramallah. He was lucky to get a hearing so early, she was told. Other parents waited for three, four, and five months before their children were brought to trial and they could see them.

Huda was instructed to come early for a thorough security check. After waiting for several hours, she entered a cramped courtroom. Only the military judge, the prosecutor, Hadi, his lawyer, a translator, and a few soldiers and security officers were present. The chances of Hadi being released were nonexistent; the military court's conviction rate was 99.7 percent. For children charged with throwing stones, the rate was even higher: of the 835 children accused in the six years following Hadi's arrest, 834 were convicted, nearly all of whom served time in jail. Hundreds of them were twelve to fifteen years old.

Just before the hearing began, Huda learned that Hadi had confessed to throwing stones and writing anti-occupation graffiti. She was told that it was forbidden to speak to Hadi or attempt to touch him—the judge would throw her out if she tried. When Hadi was brought into the courtroom, he was chained at the leg to another prisoner. Huda managed to stay silent but gasped softly as she saw a large burn mark on his face. Now crying, Huda stood up and through the translator demanded a halt to the proceedings. She was a doctor, she said, and could see that her son had been tortured.

The IDF judge barked at her to be quiet and sit back down. Huda refused, insisting that Hadi lift his shirt and lower his pants so the court could see that his confession had been extracted under torture. The judge allowed it. Hadi's body was covered with bruises, as if he had been beaten with batons. Huda shouted that the soldiers who tortured him should be tried. As the judge adjourned the hearing, Huda rushed to her son, ignoring the yelling of the guards, and gave Hadi the hug she had suppressed on the night of his arrest. She imagined warming him with her hug ahead of his stay in the cold prison cell. The judge bellowed: this would be the last time she would touch her son until he was released.

Hadi's lawyer, who encouraged the family to take whatever deal was offered, brought a proposal for nineteen months in jail, with a reduction to sixteen months for a fee of 3,000 shekels, just over $1,000. The sentence was lighter than that received by some of Hadi's friends and classmates; about twenty of them, ranging in age from twelve to sixteen, had been arrested at the same time. A number of the students had blue IDs, and their sentences were roughly twice as long as the others. There was a condition attached to the deal: Huda had to drop any claims against the soldiers who had tortured Hadi. In any case, the lawyer said, there was no chance of the soldiers being prosecuted. No one would testify against them. Hadi took the deal.

He was transferred to the Naqab prison, where Huda visted him as often as she could. Whatever she brought for Hadi, she would bring for the other inmates as well. They were teenage boys, many of them quite poor. On her UNRWA salary, she could afford to give them gifts that their parents could not. She brought books, hoping they would help keep up the boys' spirits. Hadi's friends would tell her the names of the girls they loved, and she came back with the initials inscribed on grains of rice. On one holiday, she arrived with a tapestry of a blue sky and stars for the ceiling of their tent.

Huda spent nearly twenty-four hours traveling for each short, forty-minute visit. The relatives would sit on one side of a glass partition, the prisoners on the other. Some inmates were not permitted visits by their wives or parents or children over fifteen, and others were forbidden visits altogether. The prisoners and their relatives would speak to one another through a small hole in the glass, the voices barely audible on the other side. Only young children were allowed to make physical contact. Huda would watch as mothers pushed reluctant boys and girls to embrace fathers who had become strangers. The children cried and the fathers wept, too.

Hadi's year and a half in prison was the hardest stretch of time in Huda's life, harder even than witnessing the bloodshed and grief in Tunis in 1985. It opened her eyes to a hidden universe of suffering that touched nearly every Palestinian home. A little over a year after Hadi's release, a UN report found that some 700,000 Palestinians had been arrested since the occupation began, equal to roughly 40 percent of all the men and boys in the territories. The damage wasn't only to the affected families, each of them grieving lost years and lost childhoods. It was to the entire society, to every mother, father, and grandparent, all of whom knew or would come to learn that they were powerless to protect their children.

XI

Nearly twenty minutes had passed since Huda and her staff had come upon the burning bus. Flames and smoke were still pouring from the smashed windows. Huda's driver, Abu Faraj, was directing traffic, keeping an open path for the evacuees and telling drivers of oncoming cars to turn back. The crowd had grown so large that Huda could no longer see the driver and the teacher she and Salem had pulled from the front of the bus.

She was focused on the children, gently carrying them with one of the UN nurses to the cars that had stopped at the accident site. Many of the drivers had volunteered to transport the burn victims and stood ready to race to the nearest accessible hospital, which, for most of them, was in Ramallah. The hospitals in Jerusalem were far better, but only those with blue IDs could reach them. A few of the drivers did have blue IDs, and some took off in the direction of Hadassah Hospital at Mount Scopus in Jerusalem. The majority, those with green IDs, went in the opposite direction, along the flooded road to Ramallah.

Nearly all the children had been brought off the bus when Salem, who had by now gone in and out of the flames several times, saw that Ula, the teacher and his partner in the rescue, was trapped beneath a front seat and her leg was burning. But by the time he got to her it was too late, she was gone. He carried Ula from the bus and placed her on the ground. Her nephew Saadi watched in the rain while a man covered her with his coat.

In all of this, Salem had felt nothing, not even as someone in the crowd grabbed at his arm and pinched him. One of Huda's nurses yelled to him that his jacket was on fire; he shouted back that it was not. The nurse put it out as he went to climb back into the bus. The few children still inside were no longer alive. The last boy Salem pulled out was facing down, crouched behind the frame of a seat. He was still wearing a backpack, which Salem held to pick the boy up.

Stepping out of the bus for the final time, Salem broke out weeping, shouting that he should have saved more. Somehow, not a hair on his head was burned. Abu Faraj stood unmoving, in shock, as if mesmerized by the flames. Huda turned to the nurse beside her and saw that her face was black and streaked by rain. She realized she must look the same.

They were soaked and bone weary and there was nothing more for them to do. When a Palestinian ambulance finally arrived, most of the injured children had already been evacuated. Huda didn't even notice it. The bus was still crackling with flames and there was much shouting and commotion. Not a single firefighter, police officer, or soldier had come.

Huda wanted to follow the children. She found her team, and they returned to the UNRWA van. Nidaa, the pregnant pharmacist, was still inside, inconsolable. Abu Faraj started dropping off everyone at home, as Huda called around and confirmed that most of the children were in Ramallah. Then she phoned her UNRWA supervisor. He didn't understand the magnitude of the accident and demanded that the team turn around and go to Khan al-Ahmar or he would cut their pay. Huda refused and said he should cut just her salary, no one else's.

After stopping for a quick shower, Huda set off for the hospital, taking the clinic's social worker with her. When they got there, word spread that Huda had been at the crash. A great many parents and other relatives sought her out, asking whether she had seen a boy with a Spider-Man backpack, a girl with her hair in yellow ribbons. Huda told them all the same thing: the children had been covered in soot and she couldn't tell what they were wearing.

Going from room to room, Huda checked on the injured children, soothing them. Since leaving the bus she had felt something nagging at her. She was sure the kindergartners had been silent, at least early in their ordeal. Now, at the bed of one girl, Huda asked her why that was, why she had heard no sound. "We were so scared," the girl said. "When we saw the flames, we thought we had died. We thought we were in hell."

PART THREE

Mass Casualty Incident

XII

On the eve of the accident, Radwan Tawam was sitting in his living room in Jaba when the phone rang. It was his uncle Sami, who owned a small bus company where Radwan worked as a driver. Could Radwan transport the kindergartners from Nour al-Houda on their class trip the next morning? Radwan was close to Sami, more like a brother than a nephew, and he always wanted to help, but he hesitated. From his home near the top of the hill in Jaba, he could hear a ferocious wind and see dark clouds overhead. A terrible storm was coming, and the local roads weren't built for such weather.

Early the next day, Sami kept calling and Radwan kept ignoring the calls. He wouldn't be strong-armed into driving in this weather. But not long after the last call, Sami pulled up outside Radwan's house, driving a beat-up, twenty-seven-year-old bus with fifty seats. He got out, walked past the olive and fig trees in the front yard, perpetually covered in dust from explosions at a nearby limestone quarry, and rapped at Radwan's door. Reluctantly, Radwan agreed to go.

He drove away from the house, slowly steering the bus

downhill through Jaba's narrow roads, which overlooked Tawam family land that had been seized for the settlement of Adam. During the Second Intifada, Israel had closed the main entrance to Jaba, blocking it with mounds of earth that had since become a permanent barrier. To get to Anata, Radwan and Sami first had to drive in the wrong direction, into a-Ram, then double back toward the checkpoint on the Jaba road.

At Nour al-Houda, Sami jumped out, telling Radwan he had to take care of some other business. Radwan saw a line of children waiting to board another bus, also one of Sami's, which was now overfull. So the second driver told some of the kindergartners to get off his bus and board Radwan's instead. With the rain coming down and the teachers herding damp, excited children on and off buses, no one thought to revise the passenger lists.

The students piled on and pushed past Radwan, their backpacks too large for their small bodies. As the bus left the school, the separation wall visible through the windows, Radwan turned on the television hanging above the aisle and played some cartoons for the children to watch. When he reached the Jaba checkpoint, the rain turned heavy and loud. The creaky bus was slow, so Radwan stayed in the right lane, allowing other cars to pass as he wended his way up the hill. At 8:45 A.M., less than a minute after crossing the checkpoint, the bus was struck by a massive force. Radwan blacked out.

A video taken by one of the onlookers shows the scene in the final minutes of the rescue, just before the arrival of ambulances and firefighters. In it, people are rushing to the overturned bus, which is reduced to a burning chassis, as tall red flames shoot into the air and the sky turns black with great swells of smoke rising above the rocky cliff. A woman is heard shrieking. Someone yells, "There are kids inside!" And then, "Fire extinguishers! Fire extinguishers!" A number of men fetch small fire extinguishers from their cars, and others are running with water bottles, pouring them into the blaze to no effect.

The flames grow. One man paces in a circle, gripping his face with his hands. Another hits himself on the head. A third, his fire extinguisher emptied, storms away from the bus, yelling, "Where are you people? Dear God!" He then lifts the extinguisher above his head and slams it to the ground. A small corpse lies in the road. "Cover him, cover him!" a voice calls, and then, "Where are the ambulances?" "Where are the Jews?"

Two men run forward holding a child. "The boy is alive! Quick! He needs resuscitating!" Someone else points to an adult figure on the ground. "Bring a car! This man is alive!" A blurry figure jogs away from the bus carrying a girl, her hair in braids fastened with pink ties. She seems unhurt and in a kind of trance, not answering when the man sets her down and says, "Do you need anything, dear?" More children enter the screen, one by one, and are taken to the cars nearby. Through the smoke comes the sound of wailing.

NADER MORRAR WAS the first paramedic on the scene. He'd received a call from dispatch at 8:54 A.M. reporting that a bus had rolled over on the Jaba road. The caller did not say whether the bus was empty or not. Nader knew the accident site—he had heard people call it "the death road." He assumed Israeli ambulances would get there first, since the road was in Area C, the more than half of the West Bank that after Oslo had remained under total Israeli control, governed by its army, patrolled by its police, and within the jurisdiction of its emergency services.

To get to the site from where he was stationed at the Palestine

Red Crescent headquarters in al-Bireh, Nader would have to drive through the walled-off neighborhood of Kufr Aqab, which in heavy rain could flood so badly that cars would be under water. Then on to the Qalandia checkpoint and the pileup on the single eastbound lane leading to the accident, about four and a half miles all told. In this weather, the journey would usually take around a half hour.

To his surprise, he made it in ten minutes. More surprising was that there were no Israeli emergency services, no army, no police. By the time Nader arrived, most of the injured children had been evacuated in cars, but he did not know that. He could see people up on the cliffs overlooking the road, waving their arms and shouting. To his left was the overturned school bus, still burning. Several bodies lay on the ground. "Mass casualty incident," Nader radioed to headquarters, calling for backup.

Nader moved with some discomfort. He had been a student at Birzeit University during the Second Intifada, when Israel had shut the main road to the school. At a protest calling for Israel to reopen Birzeit, a soldier shot Nader in the leg, fracturing his femur. It took two surgeries and a year of rehabilitation for him to recover, and he had dropped out of school. Inspired by the medical team, he enrolled to become a paramedic. A decade later, working for the Red Crescent, he was again shot in the leg by Israeli forces.

He had barely stepped out of the ambulance before people rushed at him to take the dead. The fire was now so intense there was no way to approach the bus. Two adults were lying on the asphalt, each with what looked like third-degree burns and both struggling to breathe. One was a teacher; the other was Radwan, the bus driver, who had multiple fractures and was severely burned. Nader and his driver loaded them onto the ambulance for immediate evacuation. The only option was to take them to Ramallah—if they attempted to go to Jerusalem, they could waste valuable time or even lose a patient while waiting at the checkpoints for permission to carry the victim on a stretcher to an Israeli ambulance on the other side.

For Nader, in a crisis, all the different legal statuses of Palestinians were irrelevant. The only thing that mattered was whether the patients were Palestinians or Jews. He could never, under any circumstances, bring someone Jewish to a Palestinian hospital. But he had brought Palestinians with Israeli citizenship to West Bank hospitals—and, for all he knew, he was now ferrying two more. As the ambulance rushed to the medical center in Ramallah, passing the Qalandia checkpoint with sirens blaring, Nader treated both Radwan and the teacher, giving them oxygen and stemming the loss of blood while trying to stay focused through their cries.

ELDAD BENSHTEIN HAD woken up early at his home in Tekoa, a settlement in the dry yellow hills southeast of Bethlehem. He had to be in Jerusalem's Romema neighborhood at 7:00 A.M. to start his shift at Magen David Adom, or Mada, Israel's national emergency medical service. Nestled at the foot of Herodion, the mountain where King Herod the Great built a palace fortress in his name, Tekoa offered spectacular 360-degree views of the West Bank. To Palestinians, the flat-topped peak was known as Jabal Fureidis, Little Paradise Mountain.

Eldad hadn't been born in Tekoa, not even in Israel—he had moved at age eleven from Moscow with his parents, both doctors. In Russia they had worked on ambulance crews. Eldad thought it was more exciting to be a paramedic than a doctor, and at sixteen

Jaba Road Area

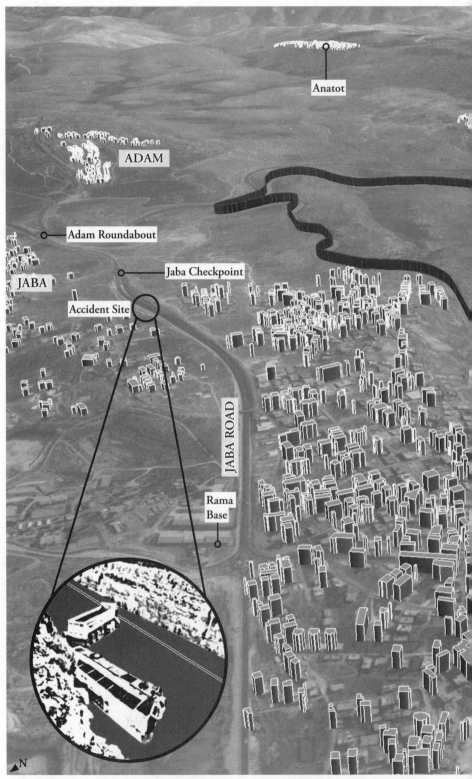

Anatot

ADAM

Adam Roundabout

JABA

Jaba Checkpoint

Accident Site

JABA ROAD

Rama Base

N

he began volunteering at Mada, years before he joined the staff. He was now thirty-three and had the look of a biker, with an earring, a shaved head, and a goatee.

His ambulance was on the way to a call in Pisgat Ze'ev, the settlement next to Anata, when the dispatcher radioed that they should change course and head to an accident on the Jaba road. Eldad knew only that the crash involved a truck. There was no mention of children or a school bus. The rain was coming down hard. With sirens on, the ambulance sped to the Jaba checkpoint, where soldiers waved them through. They first came to the giant semitrailer splayed across the road and saw fire and smoke rising behind it. As the driver squeezed around the side of the semitrailer, crowds of Palestinians up on both ridges overlooking the road shouted and gestured at them to advance. There was the bus in flames, flipped over, and there were several dead children laid out on the ground. Jumping from the vehicle, Eldad yelled in Hebrew, "Is there anyone on the bus? Anyone on the bus?" Half the people didn't seem to understand and the rest were too distressed to notice him.

It was 9:09 A.M., twenty-four minutes after the bus had crashed. Eldad was the first Israeli on the scene. Just as he got there, an army ambulance drove in from the opposite direction, coming from the Rama military base less than a mile up the road. But there were still no fire trucks in sight. Eldad went back to his vehicle to call in a mass casualty event but couldn't tell if the transmission had gone through. He tried his cell phone—no signal—then urged the army doctor to call Mada through his IDF communications system. The fire in the bus was raging and there was no way to enter it. Eldad began talking to the army doctor about triage, though with every passing moment he was more certain that any passengers left on the bus would be dead by the time the firefighters arrived.

Several minutes later, he saw Palestinian fire trucks coming from the direction of the Rama base and then he heard sirens. When more Mada ambulances pulled up—now thirty-four minutes after the crash—he asked if anyone had got his radio messages. They had, which meant additional ambulances were en route. One of the Mada drivers, an old, experienced hand, said they should position the ambulances in a single file, facing Adam, to leave room for other emergency vehicles and be ready to speed to Jerusalem as soon as they had the injured on board.

Eldad stood in the rain, watching with dread as the Palestinian firefighters extinguished the inferno. The whole thing took no more than fifteen minutes, though it felt much longer. When the last of the flames were doused, the firefighters climbed into the skeleton of the bus. The call rang out: no bodies. Eldad began to breathe again.

AFTER HE HAD carried the last child off the bus, Salem felt faint and nearly passed out. He didn't know what was wrong with him, but he didn't feel as if he could move his body. The arrival of the Palestinian firefighters seemed to revive him, and Salem began to yell. "You're an hour late!" he screamed. "You killed them! You killed our children!" He said it over and over, to every paramedic, firefighter, and police officer, whether Palestinian or Israeli.

Salem was taken to an Israeli ambulance to receive first aid and was given a shot to calm him. At first, he didn't realize where he was. As soon as he did, he ran off. Then he refused to sit in a Palestinian ambulance. "You killed these children!" he wailed again. To everyone and no one, he continued shouting that the Palestinian and Israeli rescue workers were child killers.

Israeli soldiers were at the site by this point, and one of them approached Salem. In a mixture of Hebrew and Arabic he demanded that Salem explain his accusation. The Palestinians at least had the excuse of heavy traffic from Ramallah, Salem said. And they weren't allowed to have police or fire trucks in the towns close to where the accident happened—they weren't even allowed to be on the Jaba road without Israeli permission. But still they'd arrived first. The Israelis had no excuse.

All Salem's customers at his tire repair shop were Israelis. He'd been inside their settlements for his work and he knew they had ambulances and fire trucks. The police headquarters in the Sha'ar Binyamin industrial zone was just a mile and a half away. There was a fire truck and ambulance in Tel Zion—the big ultra-Orthodox settlement above Jaba. The fire station in Pisgat Ze'ev was two miles' distance as the crow flies. He'd seen ambulances parked in Adam, less than a mile from here—so close you could see the entrance from the burning bus. The Jaba checkpoint was even closer, just down the road, near enough to smell the smoke. There was a water tank there, and the soldiers surely had fire extinguishers. How come the Jaba Bedouin managed to haul their water tanks to the cliff, but not a single Israeli soldier showed up? What about Rama, the military base? Where were the soldiers and medics and jeeps and water tanks and fire extinguishers? If it had been two Palestinian children throwing stones on the road, the army would have been there in no time. When Jews are in danger, Israel sends helicopters. But a burning bus full of Palestinian children, and they show up only after every kid has been taken away? Salem concluded. "You wanted them to die!"

The soldier shoved him, and Salem pushed him back. Within

seconds, a half dozen soldiers were beating Salem on the back of the head until he fell to the ground, and then he was punched and kicked. When the soldiers had finished with him, someone got his phone and called his wife to come pick him up. After risking his life to rescue the children, Salem spent ten days in the Ramallah hospital, with damage to both kidneys and dislocated discs in his spine.

For many months, he would wake up at night screaming, begging his wife to smell his arms, to smell the reek of death on his flesh. When he washed his hands, he insisted he picked up the whiff of burning bodies. Without warning he'd break into tears. His wife took him to a psychiatric clinic in Bethlehem. He suffered from memory lapses after the accident, and blamed them on the beating he got from the soldiers. In truth, he was grateful for the bouts of amnesia. They were the only thing keeping him from going insane.

THE MOMENT ELDAD Benshtein realized he wasn't needed, he got away from the site as fast as he could. He stopped the ambulance near Adam to smoke a cigarette and calm himself before heading back to Jerusalem. The scene he'd left—the burning smell, the charred bodies, the wailing crowd, the bones of the bus—had taken him back to his first days as a volunteer, during the 1990s, and the string of suicide bus bombings, which he had privately named the time of the flying buses.

Eldad returned to Mada headquarters and was directed to transfer one of the children from Hadassah's Mount Scopus complex to its campus in Ein Kerem. The emergency room looked like a war zone. Families blocked the hallways, holding injured children who had been brought by car and were waiting to be seen. He had been sent to pick up Tala Bahri, a girl from Shuafat Camp. He couldn't have known, but she was considered one of the most beautiful girls in the school, with large amber eyes, long curly hair, and an irresistible smile. Now she was unrecognizable— severely burned, unconscious, anesthetized, and intubated for mechanical lung ventilation.

On the way to Ein Kerem, Eldad heard on the radio that Mada ambulances were heading to Qalandia to receive patients for transfer from Palestinian ambulances, which were not allowed past the checkpoint. Most of them were injured children coming from the hospital in Ramallah because they needed better care in Jerusalem. It was only then that Eldad began to grasp the scale of the tragedy. He brought Tala to the shock trauma unit and left the ER, stepping into a small garden on Hadassah's grounds. There he stood alone and wept, for Tala, for the dead children, for the suicide bombings all those years ago.

As Eldad returned to the ambulance, a TV news crew approached him for an interview. His wife was at home in Tekoa watching the news and saw her husband, who seemed confused, struggling to find words. She had never seen him look so lost.

ELDAD HAD LEFT the accident just before a stream of soldiers, police, firefighters, and reporters descended on the site. One of the last rescue workers to show up was Dubi Weissenstern. He was used to coming in at the end. Dubi ran logistics for ZAKA, the ultra-Orthodox, or *haredi*, volunteer organization that collects the dead for burial. Its volunteers in their white coveralls would fan out over a disaster zone, combing the area for victims and scattered body parts. Nearly every one of ZAKA's Jerusalem volunteers was *haredi*, driven to fulfill the Halakhic commandments to honor the dead and bury a person intact, as they were at birth. Dubi was among the dozen paid staff members.

He had grown up in Jerusalem, studying at a yeshiva in Mea Shearim, among the oldest Jewish neighborhoods outside the Old City. Home to the most insular, stridently anti-Zionist, and predominantly Hasidic sects, its residents deem the State of Israel secular and reject its creation as a desecration of Jewish law. Dubi's family was a little more mainstream, and Dubi himself looked quite modern. He wore the standard uniform of dark slacks, white dress shirt, and black kippah, but he kept his beard in a stubble, styled his sandy blond hair like a businessman, and had cut off his sidelocks many years ago.

As a teenager, Dubi had flirted with the possibility of living a very different life. He was what was called a *shabaabnik*, a little wild, barely following the Halakha. He left the yeshiva and only half-observed Shabbat, the Sabbath. He even wanted to be a pilot in the Israeli air force, which would have made him an outcast among *haredim* and estranged him from his family. His parents said it was time to choose—he couldn't keep one foot in the *haredi* world and one foot out. Dubi jumped in, though it was not a decision made from faith. He didn't want to lose his parents.

His father and brother were volunteers at ZAKA, and Dubi joined them. They worked closely with the Israeli police and were often the only other people at a murder scene, seeing the evidence and overhearing the detectives do their work. Dubi had obtained a high security clearance and the status of a civil guard under the police. He had started work in logistics because he was afraid of seeing the dead. His best friend had hanged himself, and Dubi had been the one to find the body. He fainted at the sight and couldn't sleep for three days. As the logistics manager, he didn't go to most disaster scenes, only to mass casualty events, where he'd coordinate the volunteers and equipment.

The core principle of the work was *k'vod hamet*—respect for the dead. Five volunteers were assigned to each victim, enough to carry the stretchers or body bags without dragging them on the ground. Sometimes they retrieved just body parts. Dubi had been at the aftermath of suicide bombings, where ZAKA would spend many hours at the scene, trying to collect every last scrap of remains. On days like those, he called himself a janitor.

The bombings in Machane Yehuda, the Jerusalem market, were particularly hard. The volunteers were unable to distinguish the bombers from the victims. After one suicide bombing, Dubi and his volunteers were at the Abu Kabir morgue to deliver the remains of fifteen people when the pathologist told them they had brought sixteen hearts. Dubi sometimes had nightmares of his wife and children exploding.

It was raining when he got the call over the radio about an accident near Adam. He was ready for snow, wearing hiking boots, a navy-blue sweater, and a tan winter coat. Though he didn't know whether the victims were Jews or Arabs, he understood that it was a major collision involving dead children. He was in no rush to get to the site, not until he knew the number of victims and could decide how much equipment his colleagues would need. He drove from the ZAKA headquarters at the entrance to Jerusalem and stopped at the storage facility beneath the settlement of Ramat Shlomo, picking up stretchers, bags, cleaning equipment, and white coveralls. If the coveralls got blood on them and one of the victims was Jewish, they would need to be buried with the dead.

When he arrived at the site, the road was lined on both sides with emergency vehicles, army jeeps, and police cars, leaving an open path through the middle. Dubi took in the tractor trailer, the burned-out bus, the children's backpacks. Even with all the carnage he had witnessed, this crash was one of the worst. He knew he would look at his children leaving for school and think of the small, scorched backpacks.

Bentzi Oiring, the head of ZAKA in Jerusalem, had got there before Dubi. Bentzi was a giant bear of a man, with a large belly and a bushy gray Santa beard. With his glasses, black felt kippah, black vest over his tzitzit and white collared shirt, he seemed dressed more suitably for the yeshiva. He had worked at ZAKA since its founding in 1989 and estimated that he had been at the scene of 99 percent of the bombings in Jerusalem. Far more than Dubi, Bentzi was an anti-Zionist—he'd have no problem living under a Palestinian prime minister, so long as he wasn't persecuted and coerced into changing his lifestyle, as secular Zionist leaders tried to do.

To Bentzi, few things were as challenging as handling the dead. ZAKA stayed with the bodies for hours and sometimes days, speaking with the police, the pathologists, and the members of the *chevra kadisha*, who ritually purify Jewish corpses before burial. The hardest work was informing the relatives. Worse than seeing a dead person, Bentzi thought, was watching a family crumble before you. Those people never forgot his face, the face of the angel of death. One day in a *haredi* neighborhood of Jerusalem, a father noticed Bentzi and ran across six lanes of traffic to escape him.

After Dubi brought large blue cases of equipment, he and Bentzi and half a dozen volunteers put on latex gloves and neon yellow ZAKA vests with silver reflective stripes. Dubi stood atop an army jeep beside a soldier so that he could see above the crowd and call out instructions. Bentzi and the other ZAKA workers combed the bus, truck, and pavement for body parts. They found nothing. Dubi went after them to double-check. Someone suggested that there could be corpses trapped under the side of the bus, so they waited an hour for a crane to come and lift it.

Unlike Bentzi, Dubi refused to speak with families of the dead. He said he wasn't an actor and couldn't lie to them about what their loved ones had looked like. It was natural, he thought, that the death of Jews had more of an effect on him than the death of Palestinians—any Jew claiming otherwise had to be lying; it just wasn't the same. But even a remote tragedy took its toll. The children on the bus were part of what Dubi called a distant circle of connection, yet those backpacks had brought them closer—he could imagine himself in the place of the parents from Anata and Shuafat Camp. All deaths are devastating, even when they are expected, even when someone's sick and they have a fifty-fifty chance of surviving. But to go from zero to one hundred, that was something else. Any parent would be torn in two.

COLONEL SAAR TZUR was close to the scene of the accident, near the Qalandia checkpoint, when he first got word of it. A rising star in the IDF, he was commander of the Binyamin Brigade, which covered the central West Bank, including the greater Jerusalem region. After spending many years posted in the area, he knew it well and was now headquartered at the Beit El base at the edge of Ramallah. If anyone asked him how long he'd served in his current position, as commander, he'd say four years, not two, because he lived at the base and barely slept. On a typical day he went to bed at 5:00 or 6:00 A.M. and woke up at around 9:00 A.M. He rarely saw his wife and three young children.

The Qalandia checkpoint was a place he could never forget.

In 2004, he had pulled up in his jeep at the same time as a man from Jenin, who had been sent there by Fatah's al-Aqsa Martyrs' Brigades with a bomb. When the man saw a group of Border Police and soldiers, he remotely detonated the bomb. Saar had just gotten out of his jeep as it exploded, sending him and three Border Police flying backward. Saar was flung thirty feet through the air, slamming his head on a car. The police officers were seriously injured. The only people killed in the blast were two Palestinian bystanders.

These days, since the separation wall had gone up, most of the fatalities in the Jerusalem–Ramallah region were caused by car accidents. There were bad road injuries and deaths in Saar's sector every week. But right away Saar could see that the Jaba crash was extreme, in the devastation of the site, the distress of the crowd, the horror of seeing those small backpacks on the road.

Saar arrived to the sight of soldiers and Palestinians in a shouting match. He didn't know what the fight was about, but the Palestinians, who were plainclothes security officers, were not supposed to be there. This was in Area C, the part of the West Bank fully controlled by Israel.

The fight had started over the beating of Salem and then turned into a dispute over jurisdiction. The Palestinians wanted the Israeli soldiers to leave, an unheard-of request. As the two sides argued, the top brass pulled up—Ibrahim Salama, head of the Palestinian Interior Ministry in the Jerusalem area. Saar had heard of him though they had never met. Ibrahim was Abed's first cousin, but he had no idea that Abed's son had been on the bus, nor even that it had come from Anata.

It was a visit from Abu Mohammad Bahri, a grandfather of one of the children, that had alerted him to the accident. An enormous elderly man in a kaffiyeh, Abu Mohammad had been driving from Shuafat Camp to renew his ID at the Interior Ministry in a-Ram when he saw the collision, unaware that his granddaughter Tala Bahri was on the bus or that she was seriously injured. Abu Mohammad was distressed and speaking unintelligibly, but Ibrahim could make out that he had seen something terrible near the Jaba checkpoint.

Then Ibrahim's staff started talking about it. Bringing his deputies and a security detail, Ibrahim decided to see for himself what was happening. He was one of the few PA officials Israel allowed to travel in the West Bank with armed bodyguards. He needed them: among the most visible faces of security cooperation with Israel, Ibrahim had made many Palestinian enemies. Even Abed believed his cousin's work with Israelis crossed a red line. Ibrahim oversaw the recruitment of informants and arrest of militants and was always in meetings with powerful Israelis, from army generals to the defense minister, with whom he spoke in fluent Hebrew. He had been shot at more than once.

Ibrahim had the belly of a middle-aged man and the mischievous grin of a young boy. Cunning and proud of it, he liked to say he was a fox: he could bring someone out to sea and back without them realizing they were wet. He had recently married a second wife—the first one lived with his mother in Dahiyat a-Salaam, the new one with him in Ramallah, where he slept five days per week. Ibrahim liked to tell his Israeli army friends that when it came to his spouses he believed in Ariel Sharon's Gaza withdrawal policy, known as "disengagement." With the generals laughing, he'd add that he had tried and failed to bring his wives together in a truth and reconciliation commission.

Driving in two cars, Ibrahim and his entourage ran into the backup from the a-Ram roundabout, so they turned onto an unpaved path that ran parallel to the Jaba road. He had learned while in transit that the crash involved a Palestinian school bus and that parents were desperately trying to locate their children. When he reached an army roadblock, Ibrahim instructed his driver to stop the car, and he continued on foot. He was climbing down the rocky hill toward the crowd when he was waved over by an old friend, Yossi Stern, the head of Israel's Civil Administration—a successor to the military government—in the Ramallah district. Yossi was in charge of giving Palestinians work and travel permits, approving settlement building, and demolishing Palestinian homes. He was also involved in coordinating security with the PA, which is how he knew Ibrahim.

Yossi was standing next to Saar, both of them in their green uniforms. Saar had on two backpacks, with an antenna rising above his shoulder. As Ibrahim made his way to join them, he could see the fight going on between the soldiers and the Palestinian officers. Clearly, de-escalation was the immediate goal. Right away, Ibrahim ordered the Palestinian officers at the center of the dispute to leave. Then he turned to Yossi. He knew the requests he was about to make were audacious, but the situation demanded nothing less. First, to give the PA security services control of the site, even though they weren't allowed to be there. Second, to waive the need for permits for parents with green IDs and let them go through the checkpoints to Jerusalem.

It was Saar's call, and he agreed, without even checking with his commander. It was the first and only time Saar saw the army relinquish control in Area C. Had the victims been Jews, it would have been out of the question—and Ibrahim would never have even asked. The army would help with whatever was needed, Saar told Ibrahim. He then withdrew his troops to the perimeter, handing authority to the plainclothes Palestinian officers and firefighters. Later they were joined by the PA police, who had been held up

at the Beit El checkpoint, waiting for Israel's permission to leave
Ramallah.

ASHRAF QAYQAS, THE driver of the semitrailer, was brought to
Hadassah Hospital at Mount Scopus. He was only lightly injured,
and police investigators were able to question him at the hospital
that same day. Ashraf used to live in Anata—across the street
from Abed—and before becoming a truck driver, he had worked
with a Bedouin friend of Abed's repairing and reselling old Israeli
cars.

That morning, Ashraf had left home at 6:00 A.M. for his job
as a driver for a concrete factory in Atarot, a settlement industrial
zone in East Jerusalem. By 6:30, he was in the empty semitrailer
on the way to a limestone quarry near the Kokhav HaShahar settlement, twenty-nine miles away. He picked up a load of aggre-
gate, delivered it to the Atarot factory, and then headed back out
to the quarry for another load.

Kokhav HaShahar had been established as a military outpost
in 1975, under a Labor government, on land seized by military
order from the villages of Deir Jarir and Kufr Malik, and was
turned into a civilian settlement five years later. The Kokhav
HaShahar quarry was one of ten that were Israeli-owned in the
West Bank. In 2010, settlement quarries transferred 94 percent of
their natural stone product to Israel, accounting for a quarter
of all mined materials consumed inside the state. The remaining
6 percent went to West Bank settlements, Palestinian construction, and the Civil Administration.

Just seven weeks before the accident, Israel's High Court of
Justice had ruled on the legality of the settler quarries in the
West Bank. International law prohibits an occupying power from

plundering the resources of the occupied. Pillage is a war crime. But the court ruled unanimously that the state was permitted to exploit the West Bank's natural resources. The reason given by its president, Dorit Beinisch, who was considered a liberal justice in Israel, was that the occupation was so long-standing that it required the "adjustment of the law to the reality on the ground."

In his room at Hadassah Mount Scopus, Ashraf told the police investigators that he didn't know how the collision had happened. He couldn't say why he had driven into oncoming traffic or what had caused him to go well above the speed limit in awful weather—he had been driving at nearly twice the permitted speed: ninety kilometers on a road with a fifty-kilometer-per-hour limit. The rain had been coming down so hard he could barely see a few dozen feet ahead of him; his windshield wipers were at the highest setting and still they didn't clear his view. He had tried to slow down as he approached the Jaba checkpoint. He hadn't seen the bus, he said, because he had been looking at the road to avoid the potholes, which could have damaged the truck.

In fact, Ashraf had been grossly negligent. During a terrible storm, he had driven a thirty-ton, eighteen-wheel killing machine on a wet, declining slope at great speed. He also had twenty-five earlier traffic offenses, had limited experience operating heavy vehicles—he'd obtained his license only the previous year—and had been working for the concrete company for just one month. The company had been negligent, too: it hadn't trained Ashraf properly in the use of the very complex braking system on the truck, a ten-wheel top-of-the-line Mercedes-Benz Actros cabin connected to an advanced eight-wheel trailer.

Ashraf denied—but in subsequent testimony admitted—that when he had entered the a-Ram roundabout he might have applied a retarder, a braking device, and neglected to turn it off.

The retarder, Ashraf explained, would automatically engage as soon as he lifted his foot off the gas to slow down. He failed to mention that the manual for the truck contained a bold warning in red not to use the retarder in wet conditions, where it could cause the drive wheels to lock and skid.

Later, another police investigator asked Ashraf one final question: "You're a professional driver. In the rain can you drive with a retarder?"

"Yes," Ashraf answered. "There's no problem with it in the rain, but you have to be cautious with it."

In their report, the police concluded that Ashraf's speeding, lack of training, and inexperience with the truck's deceleration system was what had caused the accident. A driver with experience, it stated, would know that you cannot apply a retarder on a wet road.

Ashraf had been on a long, straight stretch when he lost control. As the truck veered into the two lanes of oncoming traffic, the jackknifed trailer began careening across the entire width of the road, banging against the cabin. The truck kept moving toward the school bus, its trailer swinging wildly. Although the bus slowed down and pulled to a near stop on the sloped shoulder, it was in the path of the truck. The truck struck the front of the bus, shoving it backward, and then continued to spin around in a circle, its trailer fanning out behind it. A moment later the trailer slammed into the bus and flipped it over. The impact caused a short circuit in the bus's fuse box, igniting a fire that was fanned by the day's strong winds.

At a hospital in central Israel, Radwan Tawam lay in bed, groggy from the painkillers. He had blocked out the collision, the fire on his legs, Salem and Huda pulling him through the broken front window, the twenty minutes on the ground until Nader Morrar arrived, and the agonizing ambulance ride to the Ramallah hospital. He had no memory of seeing his wife in tears by the elevators or of his brother telling the doctor there was no way he was going to amputate Radwan's legs at that crappy place. He had no recollection of his brother using connections to get him transferred to Tel Hashomer Hospital near Tel Aviv or of his cousin, a dentist, riding with him as Radwan repeated, "It's not my fault, it's not my fault."

What he remembered was waking, after a two-month coma, and finding that he had no legs. The shock triggered a stroke and a heart attack; the doctors induced a second, monthlong coma. When Radwan came around again, three months after the accident, he had lost the ability to talk. Learning that six children and one teacher had died, he broke down. After many months of rehabilitation, he was able to speak through one side of his mouth but with a slur. The hardest part was not the wheelchair itself but his humiliating, infantilizing dependency. At first he refused to wear diapers, trying and failing to go to the bathroom on his own. When the doctors took the cast off his arm, they saw that the hospital in Ramallah had set it incorrectly, leaving a large bump on his wrist. That he survived at all was due to his wife, Radwan was sure. She slept at the hospital for more than a year.

All kinds of swindlers came to Radwan, promising millions in compensation for the accident. He and his wife felt helpless dealing with Israeli lawyers and documents in a language they didn't understand. One of his sons worked at the SodaStream factory in the settlement industrial zone of Mishor Adumim, next to Khan al-Ahmar. His son's manager, who had a blue Jerusalem ID, spoke good Hebrew and offered to help. But after they gave him money to hire a lawyer, he ran off with it. Radwan heard he had moved to Beit Safafa, on the other side of the wall. With no way to go to Jerusalem to find him, Radwan gave up on getting the money back.

His working life was over, and so was his friendship with Sami, who disappeared after the accident. Radwan would spend the rest of his days confined to his home in Jaba, his wife wheeling him from room to room, the explosions from the limestone quarry sounding in the background as he watched the dust settle on the fig and olive trees in his front yard.

PART FOUR

The Wall

XIII

To Colonel Saar Tsur, the most significant aspect of the Jaba crash was that it was how he had come to know Ibrahim Salama. They remained friends, enjoying a relationship of mutual benefit. If Ibrahim asked Saar to open a Palestinian road that the army had blocked with concrete boulders or mounds of earth, Saar would do it. This kind of "easing measure," as the army called it, made an enormous difference in the lives of Palestinians, allowing them to drastically shorten their commutes, access their agricultural lands, and generally feel less entrapped. And when Ibrahim gave Saar the names of Palestinian officials and businessmen, Saar would add them to the list of VIPs allowed to exit through the exclusive and time-saving checkpoint at Beit El. Ibrahim, for his part, helped Saar reduce what the army referred to as "friction": Palestinian defiance of Israeli military rule.

For months, Saar's jeeps had been pelted with stones and Molotov cocktails as they drove on the Jaba road near the Rama base and a-Ram. Saar didn't know how to deal with it. A-Ram was a lawless area, neglected by Israel and off-limits to the PA's security forces. It was surrounded by army installations, and the separation wall tightly enclosed the whole place on three sides. Without anyone there to stop them, the residents used ladders and ropes to climb over the wall into Jerusalem.

All the measures taken by Saar's soldiers had led only to increased resistance. He directed his troops to shoot the stone-and-Molotov-throwing *shabaab* in the knees, but he was sure that one of these days his soldiers would hit higher, killing one of the protesters and further aggravating the trouble in a-Ram. Eight days after the accident on the Jaba road, that's exactly what happened. During a Friday afternoon protest at the edge of a-Ram, a twenty-three-year-old threw firecrackers at IDF troops, who shot and killed him. More stones rained down on Saar's armored jeeps.

As soon as Saar asked Ibrahim if he could do something to stop it, the problem disappeared. It never returned during Saar's tenure. Ibrahim didn't have to apply much pressure: though the *sulta* was held in contempt by the *shabaab*, it was also feared, for good reason. The experience changed Saar's thinking about how best to do his job. He concluded that he had been too reliant on military tools when he could accomplish a great deal more by exchanging favors with people like Ibrahim.

More than cooperation with the PA, Saar believed it was the wall that had made his job easier. Saar had served all over the areas under Israeli rule, and he considered greater Jerusalem and Ramallah, a single urban zone, by far the most challenging. He could hardly tell where one ended and the other began. The sector was densely populated, with Jewish and Palestinian communities right next to each other. There were Palestinians of every status, from citizens of Israel to those with blue IDs and green IDs. There were also places like Shuafat Camp and Dahiyat a-Salaam, a kind of no-man's-land, formally annexed to Israel and therefore off-limits to the PA, but totally neglected by Israeli service providers, who rarely entered them—even the fire department wouldn't go without an army escort. There was the inverse, too: settlements that had not been formally annexed to Israel but were seamlessly connected to it, receiving all the services that the Palestinians next door did not.

Because of the area's complexity and its large Palestinian population, it was a preferred route for anyone trying to carry out an attack within Israel. In 2003, a woman who had lost three relatives to Israeli fire planned to blow herself up in a restaurant in Haifa. She traveled two hours south from her home in Jenin, entered Jerusalem, and then doubled back for the two-and-a-half-hour journey north to Haifa.

The Israeli police and army argued that these kinds of attacks were proof of the necessity of a separation barrier. Saar supported its construction, especially in greater Jerusalem. He always said that there was no comparison between his stint back in the mid-2000s, when much of the wall was still being built, and later, once it had gone up in his area. In 2004 to 2006, there were three Israeli soldiers and five civilians killed in attacks in the greater Jerusalem and Ramallah region; in 2010 to 2012, there wasn't a single one.

THE SEPARATION BARRIER was the largest infrastructure project in Israel's history. At the time of the accident, it was in its tenth year of being built, and the cost had reached nearly $3 billion, more than twice the price of the National Water Carrier. Its architect was Dany Tirza, a colonel in the reserves who headed the IDF's strategic planning in the West Bank for thirteen years. He had taken part in nearly all the territorial negotiations with the Palestinians, preparing the maps for everything from Oslo's delineation of Palestinian autonomous zones to Israel's later proposals for a final agreement. Yasser Arafat called him Abu Kharita, father of the map. Dany was sure that Arafat really meant Abu Kharta, father of bullshit.

On the day of the Jaba crash, he was fifty-three years old and the head of the governing body of his settlement, Kfar Adumim. Built on land confiscated from Anata, it was established in 1979, ten years before Dany moved there. He remembered it as barren in its early years, with fewer than a hundred families and not a tree in sight. Now it was a green oasis, filled with flowers, palms, red-roofed villas, and swimming pools, and home to more than 3,400 Jewish Israelis, some of them second- and third-generation settlers. It had also expanded to create two adjoining settlements, Allon and Nofei Prat, which, with a wink, were referred to as "neighborhoods" of Kfar Adumim as a way for Israel to deny it was building new settlements.

Dany had moved to the West Bank because he wanted to be a pioneer, settling parts of the Land of Israel, just as his grandfather had done. Born in Galicia at the turn of the century, Dany's grandfather was a member of the Marxist-Zionist youth movement Hashomer Hatzair. His *haredi* family rejected Zionism and most of them perished in the Holocaust. Throughout his life, Dany's grandfather would tell his descendants that his family had died because they refused to listen to him.

Not that he had preached moving to Palestine as a safe haven for Jews. There were better places to go to flee anti-Jewish hatred. Palestine was the destination for just the tiniest fraction of emigrating Jews, a vanguard of ideologically committed Zionists. Early Zionist leaders resented the notion that they chose Palestine out of desperation rather than the idealism of creating a new nation, a new Jew, in their historic homeland. "We emigrated not for negative reasons of escape," wrote David Ben-Gurion, born in the Kingdom of Poland in 1886. "For many of us, anti-Semitic feeling had little to do with our dedication."

Dany's grandfather arrived in Palestine in 1919, when the Jewish population was less than 10 percent. When he stepped off the ship, he vowed never to leave and he held to his commitment. Despite not having very good Hebrew, he swore to speak no other language. Like many Zionist pioneers, he was fiercely anti-religious, and his son, Dany's father, had no bar mitzvah. His antipathy toward religious practice, however, did not mean spurning the Bible, which he knew well, and which even some of the most secular Zionist leaders claimed as the justification for establishing a Jewish state on a land inhabited by Arabs. "Our right in Palestine is not derived from the Mandate and the Balfour Declaration. It is prior to that," Ben-Gurion declared to a British Royal Commission. "I say on behalf of the Jews that the Bible is our Mandate."

Dany became observant at eighteen after staying at Lavi, a kibbutz founded by British religious Zionists on land belonging to the depopulated Palestinian village of Lubya, near Tiberias. He joined the army shortly after and stayed for more than thirty years, acquiring territorial expertise through his combat service and residence in different parts of the West Bank—before Kfar Adumim, he had lived east of Hebron, in the settlement of Ma'ale Hever. At the end of 1993, he was called to the office of the IDF chief of staff, Ehud Barak, who told Dany that someone with his topographical knowledge was needed to represent Israel's security concerns in the delegation negotiating the Oslo agreements.

Dany was also appointed head of what the army called the Rainbow Administration, the strategic and spatial planning unit of the IDF division for Judea and Samaria—the biblical name for the West Bank—where he oversaw the area's reconfiguration during Oslo. The prospect of a PLO-led police force operating in West Bank cities was a radical departure for Israel. To accommodate it, Dany planned a new transportation network designed to separate Jewish settlers from Palestinians, creating the bypass roads and highways that would allow Jews to travel around rather than through the Palestinian cities and checkpoints, and setting up what the army called "sterile roads" that Palestinians were not permitted to use at all.

In parallel, he devised a system of underpasses and circuitous routes for Palestinian villagers who were barred from accessing the settler highways cutting through their lands. These were given the benevolent-sounding name of "fabric of life" roads. In private, Israeli officials called them something more honest. Speaking to the US ambassador in Tel Aviv, who summarized the conversation in a diplomatic cable, Israel's deputy defense minister referred to them as "apartheid roads."

If the theme of Oslo was segregation, its symbols were the barriers that Dany built: checkpoints, roadblocks, bypass roads, and, above all, fences and walls. In 1994, the year the PA was established, Israel put a fence around Gaza and laid the foundation for what would later become the separation barrier, building the first walls in the West Bank.

Dany had expected to oversee a smooth transition to Palestinian autonomy: he thought that after six exhausting years of the First Intifada, the Palestinians were getting what they wanted—self-government, at least in the city centers of Gaza and the West Bank. But violence from Oslo's opponents, both Jewish and Palestinian, upended Dany's hopes. A few months after the ceremonial signing of Oslo on the White House lawn, a horrific massacre created what Dany called "a big *balagan*," a giant mess, making his work all the more urgent and complex.

In February 1994, a Brooklyn-born religious settler, Baruch Goldstein, murdered twenty-nine Palestinian worshippers in Hebron. Significantly, he chose to do it on Purim, the holiday commemorating the biblical story of the Jews of Persia foiling a plot to destroy them and then killing "all their enemies with the stroke of the sword, and with slaughter, and destruction." That year, Purim fell on the third Friday of Ramadan. Goldstein, a resident of Kiryat Arba near Hebron and a captain in the IDF reserves, put on his army uniform, took his assault rifle, and entered the Ibrahimi Mosque during the dawn prayers. Wearing noise-reducing headphones, he fired 111 rounds at the rows of Palestinians kneeling in supplication. The slaughter lasted for two minutes before he was subdued and then beaten to death by the crowd. His tombstone, in a Kiryat Arba municipal park, became a shrine and pilgrimage site. Its inscription reads: HE GAVE HIS SOUL FOR THE PEOPLE OF ISRAEL, ITS TORAH, AND LAND—CLEAN HANDS AND A PURE HEART.

In response, the army accelerated its push for separation, first and foremost in the place where the attack occurred. Hebron was a city of 120,000 Palestinians with 450 Jewish settlers at its center, protected at all times by three army battalions and the Israeli police. The settlers made up less than half of one percent of Hebron's population, but their presence curtailed the freedom of every Palestinian there. After the Goldstein massacre, the Jews of Hebron roamed free while its victims, the Palestinians, were subjected to day and night curfews, home raids, new checkpoints, the closure of a main market and several mosques, and prohibition from travel on the sterile roads.

The Purim bloodshed had consequences well beyond Hebron, leading, as it did, to the first bus suicide bombing, claimed by Hamas in retaliation. Many suicide bombings followed that year and in the years after, and the architecture of segregation grew. It was an irony of Oslo that those most vehemently opposed to it—Jewish and Palestinian attackers—did the most to further the process of segmentation at its core.

Dany saw his job as balancing two competing objectives: providing security for Israeli citizens while ensuring that the new infrastructure—and the settlement expansion that it facilitated—wouldn't preclude the possibility of reaching a negotiated agreement. Despite the increasing violence and the inherent contradiction in his mission, Dany still believed that peace was on the horizon. At the time, he was building a new home in Kfar Adumim. He saw no inconsistency between his role as a negotiator and constructing a house in the territory that Palestinians believed should be part of their future state. Indeed, like most Israelis, Dany assumed that Israel would keep Kfar Adumim—part of the larger bloc of settlements around Ma'ale Adumim—in any final arrangement, even though its eastern edge, the "neighborhood" of Allon, reached almost halfway across the width of the West Bank. He told himself the Palestinians could accept it: "to live a better life," he said, "it's not how much land you get but what you do with it."

The most important maps of the Oslo process, including the one that carved the West Bank into three areas—A, B, and C—were the work of Dany's hand. Drawn up in 1995, the maps designated different levels of Palestinian self-governance: in Area A, the urban zones, the PA had the greatest degree of autonomy, with jurisdiction over internal security; Area B applied to mid-size towns and villages, where Israel wished to remain fully in charge of security but found it more convenient to let the Palestinians run their own municipal affairs; and Area C, under direct Israeli administration, was for everything else: open land within, around, and between Palestinian villages; agricultural regions; national parks; Israeli military bases and firing zones; Jewish settlements, settler roads, and settlement industrial zones. Area C was not just the largest part of the West Bank—73 percent in Dany's original maps—it was the only contiguous one, an ocean of Israeli control surrounding 165 islands of Area A or B. What was once Palestinian territory dotted with Israeli settlements had been transformed by Dany's vision into its photo negative: an Israeli West Bank enveloping dozens of small enclaves of limited Palestinian self-rule. "You've turned our autonomy into a prison for us," the lead Palestinian negotiator, Abu Ala, said.

Knowing that the Palestinian delegation would object to the maps, which limited Area A to just 3 percent of the West Bank, Israel waited until the very end of the Oslo II talks before showing them. Arafat exploded. "These are cantons! You want me to accept *cantons*! You want to *destroy* me!" He stormed out of the room. The Israelis then sought to calm Arafat by offering a small expansion to Area B. Three days later, when Major General Ilan Biran, head of the IDF's Central Command, described how Palestinian police would need Israeli approval to travel outside Area A, Arafat again erupted.

> What do you think? That my policemen will be subordinate to you? That you'll humiliate my security people? That we'll ask your permission to move to a Palestinian village in B to deal with a robbery or a family spat? That's not an agreement. I will not be shamed by you! I am not your slave!

In the end, Israel got what it wanted: Arafat accepted what he had said he would reject. Palestinian space shrunk, Jewish settlements expanded, and the Oslo system, meant to be temporary, was entrenched. But Israel did not get the peace that Dany had hoped for. Within a few years, it faced a violent revolt.

The West Bank and the Wall

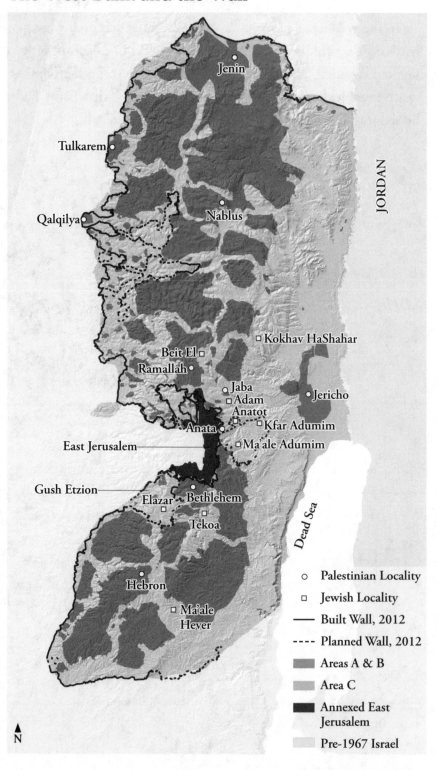

Jenin

Tulkarem

Qalqilya

Nablus

JORDAN

Kokhav HaShahar

Beit El
Ramallah

Jaba
Adam
Anatot
Anata
Kfar Adumim
Ma'ale Adumim

Jericho

East Jerusalem

Gush Etzion

Elazar Bethlehem

Tekoa

Hebron

Ma'ale
Hever

Dead Sea

N

○	Palestinian Locality
□	Jewish Locality
——	Built Wall, 2012
----	Planned Wall, 2012
▓	Areas A & B
▒	Area C
■	Annexed East Jerusalem
░	Pre-1967 Israel

XIV

Dany was charged with building the full separation wall just after March 2002, the bloodiest month of the Second Intifada. He refused to elevate the uprising by using that name, instead referring to it as the "Palestinian Terror Attack." In the thirty-one days of March, more than 120 Israelis and twice as many Palestinians were killed. Near the end of the month, a Hamas suicide bomber from Tulkarem attacked a Passover seder at the Park Hotel in Netanya, killing thirty. It was the deadliest explosion inside the State of Israel in its history. "As long as there is occupation, there will be a resistance," a Hamas political leader declared. "So we say it clearly: Occupation should be stopped and then there will be something else."

For the preceding year and a half, Dany had been tasked by IDF Central Command with figuring out how to stop the attacks, and, more specifically, prevent Palestinians from entering Israeli cities. Initially, he sought temporary solutions, believing that the intifada would pass after a few months and the two sides would resume negotiations. He was right about the renewed talks but not about the uprising. Neither the talks nor the army's responses succeeded in bringing it to an end. Dany's first project was to limit the points of entry into Jewish areas, channeling all Palestinian traffic in the West Bank onto the main roads by shutting down entrances, exits, and connective arteries with fences, gates, barriers, cement blocks, and earthen mounds. The army then quadrupled the number of checkpoints in the West Bank, stopping every Palestinian car that entered Israel, its settlements, or annexed East Jerusalem.

But the checkpoints were like gates in the desert, Dany observed. They were very easy to bypass on foot. Next the army decided to arrest and assassinate the intifada's commanders. As the resident map expert, Dany brought aerial photos of the homes of Palestinian militants when it was time for the cabinet to approve plans of attack. Within a few months, more than one hundred of the top Palestinian fighters had been apprehended. New leaders soon took their place. After that, the army shut down explosives factories, putting three hundred out of operation. Explosives didn't need to be mass produced, however. They could be made inside a bathtub or a kitchen sink.

All the while, the violence was intensifying. Dany was afraid to send his daughter to school in Jerusalem. Bombs were exploding all over: buses, cafés, markets, nightclubs, and pedestrian boulevards. Nowhere felt safe. With the country burning, there was enormous pressure on the government to do something. Both sides of the political spectrum called for separation from the Palestinians. Dany concluded that the only viable solution was to put up an extensive series of fences and walls. He and his colleagues devised plans for a separation barrier, expanding on the West Bank walls built during Oslo.

After the Passover bombing, Prime Minister Sharon decided to take up Dany's recommendation. The plan was approved by the government two weeks later. The main debate was not over whether to erect a barrier but where it would be placed. There was fear on the right and hope on the left that whatever went up would serve not as a temporary security solution but as a permanent boundary. Israel had no internationally recognized borders with Gaza or the West Bank. Even the 1949 armistice line—known as the Green Line, for the color in which it was drawn on the 1949 maps—had never been sanctioned as a permanent border. After the 1967 war, Israel prohibited printing the Green Line on official maps.

The question of how much of the West Bank would be carved off by the barrier was one of the most divisive in Israeli society. The umbrella body for settlements, known as the Yesha Council, campaigned for it to go up around the islands of Palestinian autonomy that were designated Area A. The Zionist left—and the United States—wanted something that looked less like a series of cages around Palestinian towns and more like a border fence that wrapped around the major settlement blocs but otherwise adhered fairly closely to the Green Line.

Sharon aimed to avoid the impression of drawing a final border. There would be carping from the United States and the international community if the barrier looked like an excuse for a land grab: in the early plans, 90 percent of its route strayed from the Green Line, seizing 16 percent of the West Bank for Israel. This did not include territory in the Jordan Valley—more than 20 percent of the West Bank—to be carved out by another enclosure in some of the initial plans. Sharon also worried that the settlers, for their part, would complain that the route followed the Green Line too closely, handing a victory to terrorist extortion. As a ruse, he instructed Dany to place a series of pillars in the West Bank more than a mile beyond the Green Line, to suggest that the barrier might be built there and that the actual location was merely one of several possible borders.

Within Sharon's government, there were almost as many views about the location of the barrier as there were ministers. Those who hankered for full annexation argued that the only route should be along the border with Jordan—that is, encompassing the entire West Bank. Others believed that the primary objective should be to encircle as many settlers as possible while walling off most Palestinians. The IDF chief of staff, Shaul Mofaz, echoed the Yesha Council's idea of putting walls around the major Palestinian cities. Dany was against it: he didn't think Israel could get away with placing so many people in sealed ghettos, nor did he think the plan would work: attackers could easily come from the villages outside the walls. Still other ministers lobbied for the barrier to go *inside* the Green Line, so as to place large numbers of Palestinian citizens of Israel on the same side as the West Bank. This scheme for fencing off fellow citizens was justified by the claim that many of them had protested in support of the intifada and thus their loyalty was to the Palestinian nation, not to the Jewish state.

Dany worked on the project night and day. He assembled a team of more than twenty experts—engineers, archaeologists, conservationists, environmental scientists, and Civil Administration officials with knowledge of land registration, water, electricity, and education. They went to the field to examine every inch of the proposed 450-mile route. The PA refused to cooperate with its construction, so Dany spoke directly to the Palestinian farmers and land owners whose towns and livelihoods the project would destroy.

Since the barrier would snake around Israeli settlements and Palestinian communities, doubling back on itself in some areas and creating entirely closed Palestinian enclaves in others, its route was more than twice the length of the Green Line, taking in 80 percent of the settlers. It formed a giant scar across the land. In most parts of the West Bank, it was made up of fences, trenches, barbed wire, cameras, censors, access roads for military vehicles, and watchtowers. But along more than forty miles of it—especially in urban districts such as Jerusalem, Bethlehem, Tulkarem, and Qalqilya—it was a twenty-six-foot-tall concrete wall.

XV

Like Dany, Ibrahim Salama believed an agreement between Israel and Palestine was close at hand. When Oslo was announced in 1993, he was among its strongest supporters. He told himself that cooperating with Israel would lead to the creation of a Palestinian state, which he thought not just possible but almost inevitable, and for one simple reason: it was in Israel's self-interest. This is what he would hear a hundred times from his friends in the IDF.

Ibrahim had reached this conclusion after years of pain. He had joined Fatah in 1983, at eighteen, as he was finishing his senior year at the Rashidiya school across the street from Jerusalem's Old City. He took a bus to the Allenby Bridge and then a second one to a Fatah recruitment office in Jordan, hoping to join what was left of the PLO's freedom fighters in Lebanon. It was Ibrahim's bad luck that the head of that office was a friend of his brother. The man called this brother, who said that Ibrahim going off to fight in Beirut would kill their mother. So Ibrahim was told to go home. Before he did, though, the recruiter gave him a letter to give to an underground Fatah leader in the West Bank.

To Ibrahim, the letter was a lifeline to his future in Fatah. He folded it over and over into a tiny square and wrapped it in plastic, which he sealed with a cigarette lighter. Ibrahim swallowed the tiny package and headed home. But at the Allenby Bridge crossing, he was arrested and taken to the Moscobiya detention center. The Israelis had no information on him, so he was released after a week of interrogation. Meanwhile, the letter had come out twice. Both times he dug it out of the toilet, washed it in the sink, and swallowed it again.

By the time of the First Intifada, Ibrahim had risen in Fatah's ranks, leading the student council at Hebron University to its first victory against the Islamist list. He had joined the regional Fatah committee for Jerusalem and was active in the uprising's Unified National Leadership. Inevitably, Israel arrested him early in the intifada, charging him with throwing a Molotov cocktail at an Israeli bus in Shuafat, recruiting for Fatah, forming military cells, and participating in the UNL. He was sentenced to ten years and spent more than a year of it in solitary confinement in the Be'er Sheva prison.

He was in a tiny cell, barely bigger than a bed, with a single small window in the door to receive his food. While there, seven thousand Palestinians in jails across Israel and the occupied territories launched a collective hunger strike over poor conditions and the use of solitary confinement as a punishment. Ibrahim led the strike in Be'er Sheva. It was a historic success: at the end of it, the Israeli prison service agreed to close one of its solitary wings, end strip searches, allow cooking inside the cells, and lengthen the duration of family visits.

Being in solitary had put Ibrahim under severe psychological stress. Though he had never prayed before, he started beseeching God. In his tiny cell, he tried making his heavenly appeals while standing, sitting, lying on one side and then the other. Nothing worked. It was around then that he began to question his old beliefs, concluding that there was no military solution to the conflict. In the first months of Oslo, he was released early, after serving six years and two days. In jail he had been in charge of investigating collaborators with Israel. Now he would be investigating those who resisted it. He joined one of the *sulta*'s newly formed intelligence branches, the Preventive Security Organization, as soon as he got out.

After a few years in Preventive Security, Ibrahim was transferred to the PLO's Department of Refugee Affairs. There, he came into contact with Ron Pundak, a mild-mannered Israeli policy analyst who had colaunched the first secret talks that led to Oslo. Ron worked at a think tank, the Economic Cooperation Foundation, whose self-described core belief was "that the fulfillment of the two-state solution is critical for Israel to remain a democratic and Jewish state." Although settling the West Bank had been Israel's primary national project for decades, supported by every Israeli government, whether center-left or right, Ibrahim's friends in the IDF claimed that the policy was really an aberration, driven by a small group of religious fanatics who were not representative of the state. Ibrahim believed them.

XVI

In many ways, the Adam settlement was typical: it sat on a hill-top, claimed a historic connection to a biblical site, occupied confiscated Palestinian land, inserted a wedge between Palestinian villages, had been established with the support of the Israeli government and the taxpayer-funded World Zionist Organization, and offered more affordable homes than could be found inside the Green Line—spacious single-family villas with yards and bucolic views. But in one way, Adam was unique among the settlements: it had been created by poor Mizrahi Jews, immigrants from the Middle East and North Africa.

Its fifty-nine-year-old founder, Beber Vanunu, had been raised in a Jerusalem housing project filled with new arrivals from Arab states, especially Moroccans, who formed Israel's largest Mizrahi community. He had been born in Casablanca in 1952, two years before his family came to Israel. Morocco had not wanted the Jews to leave—had in fact attempted to limit their exit—but Beber's parents emigrated anyway, out of Zionist conviction.

They were gravely disappointed. Israel placed the Mizrahim in *ma'abarot*, densely packed transit camps where they slept in tents. The camps were fenced-in and guarded by police, who prevented the immigrants from leaving. They lacked running water, adequate sanitation, and trained teachers for the children. Israel's Ashkenazi elite treated the Mizrahim with contempt. Eleven of the twelve ministers in the first Israeli government were Ashkenazi immigrants. At a cabinet meeting, Prime Minister David Ben-Gurion proposed building outhouses for the Mizrahim instead of bathrooms. "These people do not know how to make hygienic use of a toilet in the home," he said. Unemployment rates were high, as was the incidence of tuberculosis, polio, and infant mortality. Thousands of children died.

Parents of more than a thousand Mizrahi children accused the government of falsely reporting their babies' deaths and then secretly handing them to Ashkenazi parents wishing to adopt. They were never allowed to see their children's bodies, burial sites, or death certificates. Beber was told that a younger sister was stolen at five months old. Decades later, the Health Ministry confirmed some of the accusations in an internal report; Israeli officials had justified the deceit on the grounds that the Mizrahim were "backward" and the abductions were in "the best interests of the children."

Although Ben-Gurion disdained the "primitive Jews" from Arab countries, the Mizrahim were also considered necessary for the success of the Zionist project. "Had we not brought 700,000 Jews in then without thinking about it twice, 700,000 Arabs would inevitably have returned," Ben-Gurion said. "We blocked the way for them." After leaving the transit camps, some of Beber's relatives moved into houses that belonged to Palestinians who were now forbidden to return.

Beber would always resent the poverty of his youth. His family lived ten to a room in their Jerusalem tenement. When he got home at night, he had to step over his brothers to get in bed. His father, who knew several languages, was passed over for a government job by a recent Polish immigrant who didn't speak Hebrew. His mother, who read and wrote in French, worked as a cleaning woman at a Jerusalem health clinic.

The slums where Beber was raised were filled with crime and drugs. When he got involved in rehabilitating his neighborhood, he saw that big contractors were making huge profits on the renovation. Instead of giving jobs to locals, they preferred to bring in low-paid Palestinian laborers from the West Bank. Beber let the contractors know that they weren't welcome. Some protested, but they all realized what would happen to their equipment if they didn't listen. After the contractors left, the local residents were hired to do the work. Crime and drug use went down. Beber saw joy on the faces of some of his neighbors for the first time.

In the 1970s, Beber had been a member of the Black Panthers, a Mizrahi empowerment movement modeled on the African American group of the same name. The founders all came from Moroccan families. Growing up, Beber had watched as the state gave free land to the Ashkenazi kibbutzim, enriching their members. He knew he wouldn't get a shot at that. His father used to say that they wouldn't make him prime minister even if he was the last person left in the country. For a Mizrahi Jew to get anything, he'd have to take it. At the end of 1982, Beber decided he would build a town for his people, just like the Ashkenazim did. He went to see Anatot, a new settlement outside Jerusalem, pretending he was interested in living there. What he really wanted was to know how to set up a community of his own.

Beber watched and learned. The next summer he and a few other families from his slum put up tents on the road to Jericho, near the site of the Inn of the Good Samaritan, where an

Ottoman khan once stood. The army wanted that land for itself, so it offered Beber and his friends a site on the other side of the road, on Anata land. Soldiers from the Beit El base brought them caravans, water tanks, a generator, and gas stoves. But it didn't last long. That particular hill fell within the boundary of Kfar Adumim, whose Ashkenazi settler residents wanted it for their younger generation.

Beber next set his sights on a piece of land belonging to the village of Jaba. Minister Yuval Ne'eman, a former theoretical physicist and head of the government's Committee for Settlement, told him to choose a different location, somewhere close to Nablus or Ramallah. Israel didn't need another settlement outside East Jerusalem, where there was already a strong Jewish presence. The priority was to go deep into the West Bank, using a military strategy of setting up an outpost at the edge of enemy territory and then solidifying control over the area leading up to it. Accordingly, new settlements were placed far away from existing blocs, with the intention of building up the area in between.

But Beber wasn't interested in strategy. He wanted to live near Jerusalem. And he thought Ne'eman was wrong: an orange is eaten piece by piece, not in one go. With a map on the desk in front of him, Beber said no to the award-winning physicist. "I'm not from the university and I didn't study at the Gymnasium," he said. "I'm from the slums"—he put his finger on Jaba on the map—"and I want to build here."

Beber got his way. The government announced a new settlement, on Jaba land, called Geva Binyamin, after the biblical town of Geva. Beber wanted a different name, Adam, in honor of Yekutiel Adam, an IDF deputy chief of staff who was killed in Lebanon and whose family was from Dagestan in the Caucasus. The government wouldn't agree. They named streets after the most insignificant Ashkenazim, Beber thought, and they wouldn't call a single settlement after the highest-ranking officer ever killed in battle. Because he was Mizrahi. Beber saw street after street called Berkovich, Meirovich, Moskovich, Bernstein, Feinstein, Weinstein, Ginzburg, Goldberg, Grinberg—and still they couldn't allow just one Adam. But Beber had the last laugh: the whole country called the settlement by its unofficial name.

Beber became head of the settlement's council. He thought of himself as having good relations with the local Palestinians, even though Adam was built on Jaba's land. He hired villagers from Jaba as domestic workers and as laborers to build out the settlement's eastward expansion. He liked to brag that in Jaba they called him mukhtar. So when he saw smoke from the bus accident, which was visible from the settlement, he rushed to the entrance gate and grabbed the security officer to drive to the scene. By this time, the ambulances and fire trucks had finished their work.

As one of Adam's most prominent figures, Beber wanted to make clear that the community took no pleasure in the suffering of its Palestinian neighbors and bore no responsibility for the crash. When he came back from the site, he got people involved in making a large banner offering condolences from the community of Adam to the families of the children. It was posted near the Jaba checkpoint, over a settler bypass road.

XVII

Ibrahim didn't know any settlers himself. But after the Second Intifada broke out, he was introduced to one by the ECF, Ron Pundak's organization. The ECF wanted to help the army contain the uprising, and one of its staffers, a battalion commander in the IDF reserves, set about brokering a pilot nonaggression agreement between a Palestinian village and a nearby settlement. Given Ibrahim's close ties to the Israeli establishment, he was entrusted with representing Anata in discussions with the settlement of Anatot.

The representative of Anatot was Adi Shpeter, a secular Romanian-born man in his midforties who was a reserve officer in the West Bank. He didn't much care for the staff at the ECF, with their patronizing, holier-than-thou attitude toward the settlers. He had moved from Jerusalem to Anatot not long after its founding in the early 1980s. At the time, it was a barren ridge with almost no infrastructure. His wife thought he was crazy. The land was stunning, though, with breathtaking violet sunsets and panoramic views of the yellow desert hills extending to Jordan. A lifelong supporter of the right-wing Likud party, he nonetheless attached no political or ideological meaning to living in Anatot. Not initially. But when the First Intifada started, he realized he was on the front lines. Anata's *shabaab* threw stones and Molotov cocktails at Anatot's cars driving on the road that ran between the two towns. He dreaded the ride back home from work every evening. The violence subsided with Oslo and then resumed a decade later with the Second Intifada. Adi carried a gun with him day and night.

In normal times, there were a few Anatot settlers who shopped in Anata, among them an Arabic-speaking, high-ranking police officer. Other nearby Palestinian villages welcomed them, too. The parents of Ibrahim's first wife had a grocery store in Hizma, and they frequently served settlers from Adam, Anatot, and Pisgat Ze'ev. Some of the settlers were such regular customers that they bought on credit, with the grocery keeping tabs for Moshe, Yair, and Avraham.

But the Second Intifada was not a normal time. Even in a quiet village like Anata, settlers could face danger. Ibrahim would get a call from Israel's Civil Administration saying that an Israeli had just driven into Anata, and he'd rush to the scene, sometimes stopping the *shabaab* from pelting a car with stones. During one Friday protest on the road between Anata and Anatot, Ibrahim walked into the crowd and said he would break the hand of anyone who threw a stone. On another occasion he even paid some of the activists to go home. Ibrahim knew they assumed he was acting on orders from the PA.

Through the ECF, Ibrahim and Adi agreed to try to curb the hostilities between their communities. Ibrahim was proud of their cooperation. He believed it saved lives on both sides. He personally rescued at least eight Israelis who wandered into Anata by accident. But he said his real motive was protecting his village. If a settler or a soldier got hurt, the IDF would invade Anata that same evening; people were likely to die. Ibrahim told himself he was acting out of a sense of responsibility for his people and the belief that Palestinians could only lose in a military confrontation, the field in which Israel was strongest.

For his part, Adi restrained the members of his community. Anatot was filled with secular, right-wing Jews, a number of whom worked in the security forces or the Civil Administration. Some of them were chomping at the bit to head out to the road with their weapons and confront the *shabaab* throwing stones and Molotov cocktails. They had once gone into Anata and shot at the water tanks on the roofs. Adi would ask them to wait, just for an hour or two, till the crowd would subside, explaining that the protesters were only young kids letting off steam. He also helped coordinate some small humanitarian gestures from the people of Anatot, like donations of canned goods and powdered milk that were sent through Ibrahim.

The two became good friends. Ibrahim brought his family to visit Adi and his wife Naama, a spokesperson at the Hebrew University. Their children played together and their wives enjoyed each other's company. Ibrahim called Adi his brother. Somehow, despite his years in prison, his family's loss of land, his basic freedoms denied, Ibrahim seemed not to resent Israelis, nor to care that people like Abed disapproved of his close relationships with them. At one point in the Second Intifada, Adi was called up to the reserves and sent to take part in the IDF's siege of Arafat's headquarters in Ramallah. Ibrahim happened to be driving to the same city when he was stopped by an IDF vehicle near Jaba. Getting out of the car, he saw that the officer in the green uniform was Adi. To the puzzlement of everyone around them—soldiers, villagers, settlers, and Palestinian drivers—Ibrahim pulled Adi into a fierce hug.

XVIII

For Dany, by far the most complicated and politically sensitive part of the barrier was in and around Jerusalem. Here, with the city's large Palestinian population, Israel's great conundrum was distilled to its essence: how to include as few Palestinians as possible on the Israeli side without conceding an inch of territory.

There were three possible routes for the wall in Jerusalem. The first was a purely demographic line that would separate the Jewish settlements from most Palestinian neighborhoods. This was a nonstarter politically because it would be seen as ceding much of Palestinian East Jerusalem to a future Palestinian state. Palestinians would have opposed it as well, not wanting to be cut off from their families, jobs, schools, hospitals, churches, and mosques.

The second option was to follow Israel's unilaterally declared municipal boundary, putting a wall around all the villages and East Jerusalem neighborhoods it had annexed in 1967. The problem with this was that large urban areas stretched across both sides of the municipal line. Building on the boundary between places like Anata and Dahiyat a-Salaam would mean bulldozing apartment buildings and cutting up neighborhoods. Also, there were some thirty thousand West Bank Palestinians with green IDs living in Shuafat Camp, Dahiyat a-Salaam, and the adjacent neighborhoods, all within the municipal boundary of Jerusalem. If the wall encompassed those residents, Israel would have to either give them blue IDs or evict them. It would mean a public relations disaster and quite possibly bloodshed.

The final option was the one Dany chose: to follow the municipal border as closely as possible, while lopping off several densely populated annexed areas, including Kufr Aqab and the entire enclave of Shuafat Camp and its surrounding neighborhoods: Ras Khamis, Ras Shehadeh, and Dahiyat a-Salaam. The de facto removal of these neighborhoods from municipal Jerusalem also served Israel's demographic goal of keeping as many Palestinians as possible out of the city.

So tens of thousands of the city's residents found themselves on the wrong side of a wall. Although the municipality remained responsible for these new ghettos, it ignored them. The Border Police prevented emergency services from entering them without an army escort. In 2006, an ambulance from the center of Jerusalem was sent to the Shuafat checkpoint to pick up a man who had suffered a heart attack on the other side of the wall. The Border Police refused to let the ambulance pass until an army escort vehicle arrived. The paramedics defied the Border Police by taking their equipment out of the van and running through the checkpoint to the man's home. They weren't able to bring him to Hadassah Hospital on Mount Scopus, just above the refugee camp, until two hours later, by which time he had died.

After the wall went up, Dany wanted to find a solution for the neglected neighborhoods on the other side. He considered recommending that the wall become the new municipal boundary—meaning that Jerusalem would no longer be formally responsible for those areas outside the wall. But what would happen to the blue ID holders in those neighborhoods, more than one fourth of Jerusalem's Palestinian population? Dany feared that any plan that involved taking away their residency rights would lead to huge numbers rushing to the Jerusalem side of the wall before the policy was implemented. The last thing the government wanted was to bring more Palestinians into the heart of the city.

Still, Dany floated the gerrymandering idea to the mayor of Jerusalem, Nir Barkat, who endorsed redrawing the municipal boundaries, only to issue a swift retraction. Right-wing politicians denounced the proposal as relinquishing Jewish sovereignty in the Land of Israel. The Shuafat Camp and Kufr Aqab enclaves remained forsaken.

XIX

B y the time Ibrahim took over the Interior Ministry branch in a-Ram, the wall had reshaped the lives of the Palestinians living on both sides of it, including his own family. The more than 100,000 people in the areas of Shuafat Camp and Kufr Aqab, who had previously received services from Jerusalem, were left without local ambulances, fire trucks, and police. There wasn't a single ATM in Shuafat Camp and its adjacent neighborhoods. Only Israel's army and Border Police entered them regularly, usually in armored vehicles, carrying assault rifles, and wearing helmets and body armor.

These enclaves became a haven for fugitives fleeing the authorities. Criminal families of '48 Palestinians moved into Dahiyat a-Salaam. Murders in the area went unsolved. An ex-head of the Jerusalem district police said of the precincts beyond the wall, "We have no need for them. . . . The Israeli police doesn't go in there." In one incident, an armed gang entered a school in Kufr Aqab, threatening the staff for several hours. Parents begged Israeli police to come, but they didn't.

The chaos spilled over to nearby communities like a-Ram and

Anata, which were also, like municipal Jerusalem, off-limits to PA security forces. Ibrahim wasn't allowed to bring in Palestinian police and fire trucks without Israel's permission. To arrest a criminal, he would typically have to wait for three or more days for Israeli approval. For anything urgent, such as stopping a feud, permission was usually granted after several hours.

The problems in the area mounted as the population ballooned. Palestinians with blue IDs who couldn't afford rent on the Jerusalem side of the wall moved into the crowded neighborhoods just beyond it. That was the only way they could keep their blue IDs. Shoddily built apartment towers sprung up to accommodate the influx. The infrastructure was collapsing. Power outages were frequent. The area was so neglected that Israel didn't know how many people were living there.

An illicit economy developed around the wall. Israelis sold expired goods to businesses on the other side. Cheap Palestinian products that didn't meet health and environmental standards went in the opposite direction. Drugs passed through small holes drilled into the barrier. Hazardous waste from Israel was dumped in Palestinian areas. Thousands of old, unsafe cars without registration were sold to Palestinians behind the wall, where neither the PA nor Israel checked their licenses.

In and around Shuafat Camp, parents took their children out of the schools in Jerusalem, afraid to put them in daily contact with soldiers at the checkpoint. There was only one city school on their side of the wall, in a former goat pen. The shortage of classrooms—more than two thousand were lacking in East Jerusalem—was so bad that pupils were forced to study in shifts. There were children at the city schools who still couldn't read at age nine. More than a third of the Palestinian students in Jerusalem dropped out before the end of high school.

There were UNRWA schools that served Shuafat Camp, but they were awful, too. Some of the teenagers were taking drugs. The most popular was "Nice": marijuana, tobacco, or other herbs covered in chemicals—pesticides, acetone, ether, rat poison—that gave off a high. From there the kids moved on to heroin, which was sold openly in the streets of the camp. The addicts were getting younger and younger, and so were the teens hospitalized for overdoses.

Parents who could afford it put their children in private schools, which were largely unregulated. In February 2012, one such school, Nour al-Houda, hired a bus company to take its kindergarten class to a play area in Kufr Aqab. The company sent an illegally registered twenty-seven-year-old bus to drive on neglected, congested roads, without proper lighting, a police presence, or a barrier between the lanes of oncoming traffic.

PART FIVE

Three Funerals

_____

XX

When Abed reached the hospital in Ramallah, he forced his way through the bedlam of shouting parents, children on stretchers, doctors, nurses, police, photographers, and Palestinian officials. He gave Milad's name at the reception desk and was told there was no information on his son. Abed began searching in the hospital rooms, where he saw many of Milad's classmates and their families. He was pleased for the parents who had found their children, although they barely noticed him amid the commotion. He asked everyone whether they had seen Milad. No one had.

Abed returned to the reception desk, saying that he had checked in every room and his son was nowhere to be found. "Your child was on the second bus," someone called over the din. "That one wasn't in the accident. It went to a-Ram." This was the first Abed had heard of a second bus. He called his friend Ziad Barq, whose child was in Milad's class, asking him to check with his wife, Mufida, the teacher who had helped Abed pay for the trip. Mufida called back right away. "Milad was on the second bus. He's fine."

Scarcely able to trust this miraculous news, he left the hospital lobby to stand for a moment in the rain outside. Soon, a parent told him that Milad had actually been transferred from Ramallah to Hadassah in Ein Kerem. With his green ID, Abed couldn't go there himself, so he called a cousin in Dahiyat a-Salaam who had a blue one. About an hour later, the cousin reported back: a few of the injured children had been admitted, but not Milad. Then Abed got word that the second school bus was on its way back to Anata. He phoned one of his brothers, asking him to go meet it. Several minutes passed and his brother returned the call: "Milad is not here."

The families were buzzing with news and rumors, which were passed on to Abed throughout the day: Milad is at the military base outside a-Ram; he's in a hospital in Israel; the army's letting Nour al-Houda parents with green IDs into Jerusalem. Abed felt as if he were being dunked in barrels of water: first boiling, then freezing. Hot, cold, hot, cold, hot again, cold again. He stayed in Ramallah, by the ER, refusing to answer the reporters who kept pestering him. His younger brother Bashir, who was a video editor at Al Jazeera, came to wait with him together with a nephew. All the while, his phone did not stop ringing, many of the calls from journalists and radio stations. Abed wouldn't speak to them—he was too anxious. He gave the phone to Bashir, telling him he would talk only to Haifa.

But when Haifa called, she had no news, either. She was waiting at home with Adam and Abed's four daughters. The eldest, Lulu, now sixteen, had been the first to come home that morning. She was like a mother to Milad, putting him to bed each night. She was often the one to wake him and help him get ready for school. But the day of the trip was a special occasion, and Haifa had dressed and fed the boys herself. So Lulu had left without seeing Milad.

She had been at the Anata girls' school, around the corner,

when her teacher suddenly told all the students to go home, giving no explanation. As Lulu walked out the classroom, she overheard another teacher saying there had been an accident. At her house, she learned that the crash involved the Nour al-Houda kinder-gartners, but Haifa insisted that Milad was okay. As news came in from neighbors and the television, Lulu grew increasingly agi-tated and kept asking Haifa to call Abed. People were dropping in—teachers, classmates, other parents—and contradicting each other. Someone claimed she had seen Milad get on the second bus. Someone else said he'd been on the first one. Another main-tained that he hadn't even gone on the trip.

Adam came home from Nour al-Houda not long after Lulu. His class had been dismissed at morning recess. He was thrilled until he saw the teachers crying and heard from a friend that Milad's bus had been in an accident. He got a ride home with Haifa's brother-in-law, who drove the boys to and from school each day. Entering the house, Adam realized that he had forgot-ten his lunch that morning and then saw it sitting on his bed. He ate his *ka'ek* with falafel, lay down, and fell asleep for the rest of day, as if his brain wanted to protect him from the worry. When he woke up, hours later, he found his four sisters crying, clutch-ing Milad's clothes and breathing in his scent.

ABED WAS SO tightly wound with fear that he hardly noticed what was happening around him. The Palestinian president and the prime minister had each come to the hospital, along with their large entourages. Abed's own cousin Abu Jihad walked right past him at the entrance to the ER. Abu Jihad's brother and brother-in-law both had children who had gone on the trip. The three men had driven to the Jaba road, but by the time they arrived, the fire was out and the students had all been evacuated. The traffic out of there was so bad that they had left their car at the side of the road and set out for Ramallah on foot. At the Qalandia checkpoint, they caught a ride to the hospital.

The staff were overwhelmed, mobbed by parents and family shouting out questions. Abu Jihad heard that some of the dead were at the hospital morgue. Eventually he was directed to a wall affixed with handwritten lists of the names of the children present and their room numbers. He found his nephew and niece on the list, Mohammad Bakr and Zeyna, and ran to their room. When he opened the door, he saw Mohammad Bakr holding Zeyna's hand.

She was dark with soot from head to toe. Her skull was fractured and her hand was broken. Mohammad Bakr said he had been sitting at the front of the bus when it crashed, but he immmediately moved toward the back and found Zeyna trapped under a piece of metal. He helped pull her out from under it. Abu Jihad ran to the lobby to get his brother—Zeyna's father—who was slumped on the floor, sure he had lost his daughter.

Abu Jihad was back at Zeyna's bedside when Abu Mazen, the Palestinian president, came into the room, followed by camera crews and photographers. At seventy-six, he had a grandfatherly bearing and a full head of white hair. He stopped to talk to every kindergartner, exchanging a few words. As he left each child's bed, the cameras would linger on an aide handing over a toy in a large shopping bag. Some of the children got home to discover that their gift, a PlayStation, was broken.

At Zeyna's bed, Abu Mazen turned to Abu Jihad. "How are things in Anata?" Abu Jihad was perhaps the only Salama who had even less respect for the PA than Abed did. A local leader of Islamic Jihad, he saw the PA as a source of persecution. "All of

Anata is *zift,*" he told Abu Mazen, using a word for asphalt that also meant crap. "Except for the streets, since none of them are paved." Abu Mazen laughed. Abu Jihad then complained about the complete lack of services in the town—not even a bank or a clinic. "No one cares about us," he said. Abu Mazen promised he would take care of it, then left for a photo op near the hospital entrance, where he donated blood.

BY LATE AFTERNOON, most of the parents had located their children. Only Abed and a handful of others had not. Abed did not know that six bodies were at the hospital, lying in the room next to him. One was the teacher, Ula Joulani. The other five were children. Three were too badly burned for identification. The remaining two, a girl and a boy, were not. Although he felt useless at the hospital and wanted to search for his son in a-Ram and Anata, Abed had a strong feeling that Milad was nearby. Something told him not to leave.

The parents who had reunited with their children began to depart, which is when Abed learned from the hospital staff about the bodies in the adjacent room. He desperately wanted to go inside. His nephew urged him not to. A doctor came out of the ER, looking for parents to identify the two recognizable bodies. He asked Abed for the color of his son's hair. "Blond," Abed replied. "You need to stay here," the doctor said. "This boy has black hair." The doctor turned to a father standing beside Abed. His son had dark hair, and he was permitted to enter. He came out screaming and hitting himself in the head.

In that moment, Abed confronted the very real possibility that Milad's body was in the room, burned beyond recognition. Another doctor came to take blood from Abed to test for DNA and told him to call his wife and son to also give blood samples. Abed phoned Haifa, who left with Adam right away. Waiting for them beneath the fluorescent lights of the hospital hallway, Abed cried and prayed on the linoleum floor.

Abed hadn't told Haifa and Adam why they were needed at the hospital. Haifa walked in with a look of shock on her face. Adam seemed utterly bewildered. Abed thought how young and helpless his nine-year-old son appeared—too young to be witnessing this scene. They all joined the doctor in a room off the hallway where Abed had been praying. Adam was crying, and the doctor asked if it was because of the needle. Adam shook his head.

Once the DNA tests were over there was nothing to do but wait. Bashir drove them home. The house was full of women—family, neighbors, and friends. Haifa barely spoke. Bashir's wife, Ruba al-Najjar, noticed that Haifa wasn't crying and offered her a cigarette. Ruba told her that she should do whatever she wanted. If she felt like crying, she should cry. If she didn't, that was fine, too. Haifa said that she was okay.

Ruba knew that kind of silence. When she was sixteen, her brother had been severely beaten under interrogation and was temporarily paralyzed. As soon as she heard the news, Ruba went out to stab a soldier. In the Old City, she injured a border guard near one of the gates to al-Aqsa. She was arrested and sentenced to three years in prison, which is where she was when her father died in an accident. Ruba was taken out of prison by the guards for a visit home. Although no one told her the reason for the visit, she knew it could only be that someone in her family had died.

After, on the return journey, she held on to a photograph of her father. The soldiers began to sing in Hebrew, "I love my faa-ther! I love my faa-ther!" They sang the same line over and over, loudly, joyously. Ruba determined to do whatever it took not to let them see her cry. I am a stone, she told herself. When she got back to the prison, she had lost the ability to speak. Women in the jail tried to help by pinching and scratching her, forcing her to yell. After a few days of silence and a strong twist on her ear, she yelped in pain and began to sob. She could speak again.

Smoking a cigarette beside Haifa, Ruba realized that it had been nearly twenty years since she went mute. She still cried when she talked about the cruelty of the soldiers and the force of will she had summoned to hide her pain. Ruba didn't want Haifa to lose her ability to speak too.

ABED HAD JOINED some men at the Anata Youth Club up the hill, sitting with them until around midnight. When he returned to the house, the living room was still filled with women, talking softly and listening to a radio recitation of the Quran. Although he knew that Milad coming home became less likely with every passing minute, Abed still held out hope that his son might be alive. There were more parents missing children than there were bodies in that room; some mothers and fathers had only just located their children, fifteen hours after the accident. Perhaps Milad was at the Israeli military base, after all. Perhaps he was at a different hospital. Maybe one of the people who had taken the children in their cars had brought Milad to their home in a-Ram or Jerusalem, where their family was now feeding him and trying to find his parents.

Abed went to the bedroom, where Haifa was sitting on the bed talking to her sister. Normally, Milad would be sleeping there between his parents. At the sight of the empty bed, Abed broke down. He entered the bathroom, shut the door, and wept loudly.

It was the first moment he'd had alone since hearing the news that morning. Haifa heard him crying and came to the bathroom. She held Abed's heaving body, comforting him. Sobbing in her arms, Abed thought it should be the other way around—he should be comforting Haifa. But she hadn't shed a single tear.

XXI

Nansy Qawasme was among the youngest mothers at Nour al-Houda. She was just twenty-three, having married in her final year of high school, at seventeen. She had spent her early years in Hebron, where her father was from, and then moved to her mother's Jerusalem neighborhood of a-Tur, on the Mount of Olives, when she was eight. Her father had a West Bank ID and her mother a blue Jerusalem one. Because Nansy was young when the family moved to a-Tur, she was able to get a blue ID as well.

Nansy's husband, Azzam Dweik, was twenty-nine when they wed. He repaired air-conditioning units on buses in the West Jerusalem industrial zone of Talpiot. The marriage had been arranged in the traditional manner, after Azzam had heard about Nansy and asked his parents to meet with hers. She didn't have much of a say in the decision. Everyone around her acted as though it would be a catastrophe if she were still single at eighteen. Shortly after the engagement, she told her parents that she didn't want to marry Azzam. This wasn't the match she had imagined. But her family said it was too late: she and Azzam were not just engaged but formally married under Islamic law and her prospects would dim if she were divorced.

In advance of the proposal, Azzam had bought a second-floor apartment in one of the tall, unregulated buildings in Ras Shehadeh, next to Shuafat Camp and Dahiyat a-Salaam. The apartment was within municipal Jerusalem but considerably cheaper than other options, since Ras Shehadeh had just been severed from the rest of the city by the wall.

Nansy was used to walking around freely in a-Tur, without fear. But Ras Shehadeh was a ghetto, filled with crime and drugs, and rife with stories of kidnapping, murder, and rape. Boys in their preteens drove without a license, having no fear of encountering traffic police. The potholed, unpaved streets were lined with heaps of trash, which residents burned in dumpster fires at night. Nansy was cut off from her family, and she didn't feel safe walking alone or going to school on the other side of the wall. She was now a pregnant high school senior and exhausted by her daily routine. She had to take a shared taxi to the Shuafat checkpoint every weekday morning, where she might be held up for half an hour, then board a bus to Damascus Gate and walk to school. Often late, she explained to her teachers that she now lived in Ras Shehadeh.

Her first child, Salaah, was born six months after her graduation party. Her daughter, Sadine, came two years later. Salaah was considered exceptionally bright. By the age of two he had memorized many more words in English and in Arabic than his peers. When Salaah entered kindergarten, Nansy thought he had the mind of a boy of ten or eleven. She decided to send him to Nour al-Houda because it was the best school in the area, and there was no other acceptable choice. She didn't want him to go through the checkpoint each morning, which ruled out the city's public schools, save for the one in the former goat pen. Many of the parents behind the wall felt the same way, spending $1,000 or more per year on private schools like Nour al-Houda. It was the only way to avoid the checkpoint.

Nansy always worried about Salaah's safety. She was afraid whenever she left him, imagining that he would get lost or fall from a height or suffer some other sort of accident. Perhaps it was because she was so young and he was her first child, but she never felt scared for Sadine. Forty days before the accident, Salaah had told Nansy that he was going to die. "I'm going to heaven and Sadine will be an only child," he said. Nansy responded that he was very young and had a long life ahead of him. But he repeated it nearly every day, torturing his mother. She was so worried that she brought Salaah and Sadine to sleep with her, telling them that she wanted to keep them warm in the winter cold.

Salaah had turned five in December. He had a party at home and another at his grandmother's, but he wanted to celebrate at school. The party kept being postponed. Every week it was someone else's birthday. Then the celebration was set for Thursday, February 16, until the class trip was rescheduled for that date. Nansy said that he would have his party a few days later. "I won't have time! I won't have time!" he screamed at her. "Either we have the party before or there will be no party." His mother caved, arranging the celebration for the week prior to the trip. He asked his grandmother to come from a-Tur. That day she took him shopping for another birthday present. He passed by all the toys in the store and selected a red and blue backpack with his favorite superhero on it, Spider-Man.

The parents had to sign a permission slip for the class trip to Kids Land. Azzam refused to sign because the weather was very bad on the Friday before. Salaah was devastated. He cried and begged, saying that he had to be there with his friends. He kept nagging Nansy to sign, and she finally relented on Tuesday morning, with just two days to go. At his grandmother's that afternoon, Salaah ate zaatar flatbread, which he had asked her to make specifically before the outing. "Why before? I'll make it after," she had said. "No," he insisted, "it has to be before." That night, Nansy bathed him, dressed him in his Spider-Man pajamas, and combed his thick black hair. As he went to sleep he hugged her and again said he was going to heaven, leaving her "alone with one daughter." Nansy felt like she was being driven crazy. "Why are you doing this to me?" she said.

The following night, on the eve of the trip, Salaah's father got home late. Salaah had kept calling him from Nansy's phone, pestering him to come home. He wanted to go and buy treats for the outing. At 9:00 P.M. Azzam took Salaah to a corner store, getting him chocolate milk, chips, and assorted candies. Salaah packed it all into his new Spider-Man backpack, which he insisted on keeping near him on the bed. He fell asleep cradling it.

It was cold and raining hard in the morning. Azzam had already left for work. Nansy stood at the window, wondering how she'd manage to wake Salaah up and send him off in this weather. It was usually hard to get Salaah out of bed. He'd stay under the sheets until the last possible moment. But this morning he couldn't wait to get out the door. He wouldn't let Nansy put on warm leggings under his gray trousers; he was too excited for even a moment's delay. She wrapped a scarf around his jacket, and together they waited for the bus downstairs. Standing outside with Salaah, Nansy felt torn. The weather seemed like anger from God. But Salaah was so happy. Nansy gave him five shekels to spend at Kids Land. "Mama," he said, "I love you very much." Then he got on the bus.

Nansy went upstairs to clean the apartment. Every few minutes she asked herself why she had let Salaah go. On days much
less rainy she had kept the children at home. Sadine didn't wake
up until Nansy had finished cleaning at around 10:00 A.M. Suddenly Nansy heard her neighbor yell. There was a knock at the
door. When Nansy opened it, two women from her building—a
mother and grandmother of kindergartners at Nour al-Houda—
were outside crying and shouting. "There was an accident," one
of them said, "and the bus is on fire." Nansy froze in the doorway.

Sadine tugged at her mother's hand. Nansy picked her up and
held her. They followed one of the neighbors into her apartment.
All of them were frantically making calls. Nansy phoned Azzam,
who hadn't yet heard the news. He was on the other side of the
wall and said he would drive to Hadassah Hospital at Mount
Scopus. The TV was on but Nansy wouldn't look at it. She was
sure that if she just went to the school, she'd find Salaah with a
light injury, maybe a broken hand at worst. She'd heard nothing
back from Azzam and decided to leave, heading downstairs with
Sadine.

Nansy's mother called before she reached the car and Nansy
explained about the accident. "Don't be scared," her mother said.
"You'll get him." In her home in a-Tur, Nansy's mother switched
the television to the news and saw images of the bus. She began to
slap her own face. A neighbor came in and asked what was going
on. "My grandson," she cried. "My grandson is on that bus."

Nansy had put Sadine in their blue Toyota and was driving
through the rain toward the school. The streets were flooded and
backed up with mud. Her tire got stuck in a pothole. She got
out of the car, crying, and ran back to their building, holding
Sadine. Just then, one of her brothers, Fadi, called and promised
to come right over. In the meantime, her neighbors had heard

that their two girls were safe. Now Azzam called from Hadassah, and her brother Osama, who worked for the UN in Ramallah, called from the hospital there. What had Salaah been wearing? they wanted to know. Nansy didn't understand the significance of the question.

Fadi arrived and drove Nansy and Sadine to Nour al-Houda. The school was empty. All the classes had been let out and the headmistress had left. Parents who had found their children were already back at home. With rising alarm, Nansy, Sadine, and Fadi drove up the hill to the Anata municipality, where they found a crowd of distraught relatives demanding news. Trying to placate the families, a man with the municipality addressed them through a megaphone. "Your children are going to be fine." A few minutes later, he added, "The children are on the way." And then: "Your children are heading back to the school." A teacher called out a list of the students on the bus, but it was wrong. It included children who hadn't even gone to school that day. Nansy wept, repeating over and over, "Where is Salaah?"

After stopping at Makassed Hospital to search for Salaah, Nansy and her family went back to her parents' apartment in a-Tur. Azzam and Osama called again—they hadn't located Salaah at any of the other hospitals but asked more questions about his clothes. Osama went into the morgue at Ramallah Hospital to check the charred bodies, a sight he wished he could forget. He wasn't sure, but he didn't think Salaah was among them. He then called around to different ambulance drivers, relaying Nansy's description of Salaah's Spider-Man backpack and clothes. Nansy remembered that Salaah was wearing blue and purple boxers with a pattern of teddy bears. One of the ambulance drivers with Mada said that a boy with that kind of underwear had been transferred to Hadassah Ein Kerem with two other children. It was late by the time Osama heard this news.

Now Nansy and her family drove from a-Tur to Hadassah Ein Kerem, arriving after 9:00 P.M., and Osama came in from Ramallah. Entering the hospital, Nansy saw practically every person she knew. She couldn't explain what they were doing there, unless they had all heard that her son was dead. She thought there must be hundreds of people. She spotted Azzam right away, but he looked straight through her. So did his parents and family. As they all waited for news, Azzam kept his distance. His family did, too. Whenever they looked at her, it was with burning hatred.

Eventually, Nansy's mother approached Azzam. "Go to your wife," she said, "comfort her."

"No, I don't want to be near her," he said. "She's the one who sent Salaah on the trip."

Greater Jerusalem

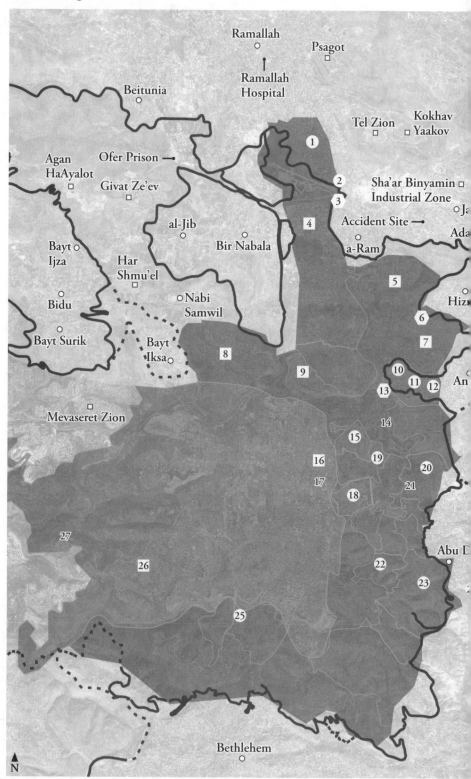

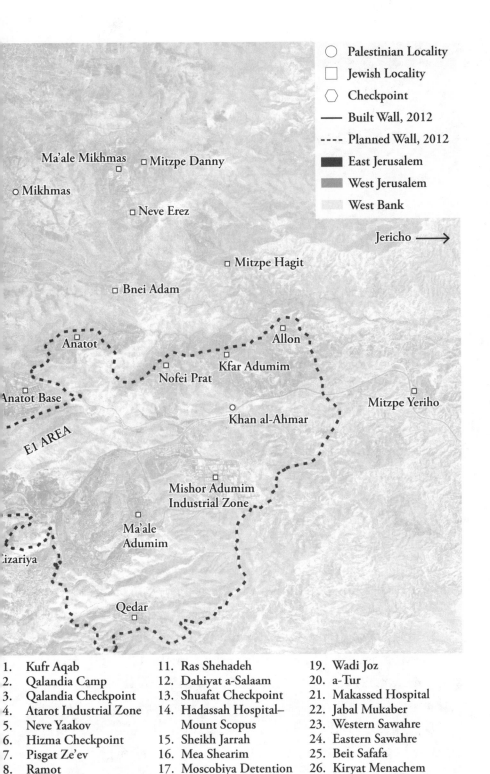

	Palestinian Locality
	Jewish Locality
	Checkpoint
	Built Wall, 2012
	Planned Wall, 2012
	East Jerusalem
	West Jerusalem
	West Bank

Ma'ale Mikhmas □ Mitzpe Danny

o Mikhmas

□ Neve Erez

Jericho →

□ Mitzpe Hagit

□ Bnei Adam

Anatot □

Allon □

□ Nofei Prat   Kfar Adumim

Anatot Base □

Mitzpe Yeriho □

o Khan al-Ahmar

E1 AREA

□ Mishor Adumim
Industrial Zone

□
izariya   Ma'ale
Adumim

Qedar □

1. Kufr Aqab
2. Qalandia Camp
3. Qalandia Checkpoint
4. Atarot Industrial Zone
5. Neve Yaakov
6. Hizma Checkpoint
7. Pisgat Ze'ev
8. Ramot
9. Ramat Shlomo
10. Shuafat Camp

11. Ras Shehadeh
12. Dahiyat a-Salaam
13. Shuafat Checkpoint
14. Hadassah Hospital–
    Mount Scopus
15. Sheikh Jarrah
16. Mea Shearim
17. Moscobiya Detention
    Center
18. Old City

19. Wadi Joz
20. a-Tur
21. Makassed Hospital
22. Jabal Mukaber
23. Western Sawahre
24. Eastern Sawahre
25. Beit Safafa
26. Kiryat Menachem
27. Hadassah Hospital–
    Ein Kerem

XXII

Hadassah Ein Kerem was the largest hospital in Jerusalem with a specialized burn unit. Livnat Wieder usually led a team of social workers in the adult oncology department, but that morning she had been called in to help with an influx of Palestinian families, most of them from East Jerusalem. She felt ill-equipped—many of them spoke no Hebrew, and she had no Arabic. She was also unused to dealing with trauma or children. Her work with cancer patients and their relatives was entirely different: long-term palliative care in which she formed close bonds with the families.

Before any victims of the crash were brought to the ER, the hospital activated its protocol for mass casualty events, which had been developed during the Second Intifada. It set up three centers: one for information, fielding calls from relatives and the media; a second for triage; and a third for family support, staffed by social workers. Hundreds of calls came in to the information center, many of them from parents with green IDs seeking permission to enter Jerusalem before the army had opened up the checkpoints to them. Hadassah staff contacted Dalia Basa in the Civil Administration, who dealt with Palestinian patients, and asked her to help with transportation and permits. Livnat was seconded to the family center, where the staff arranged tables and chairs with tea and cookies and coffee and water. All the relatives were directed to gather there. Normally each family would be assigned a social worker, but with hundreds of relatives streaming in, Livnat and the staff were swamped.

The family center had only three Arabic-speaking staffers— Huda Ibrahim was one of them. A '48 Palestinian social worker from Abu Ghosh, west of Jerusalem, she was unmarried and worked with children in hemato-oncology. Livnat adored her. She thought Huda was the best social worker in all of Israel. Huda displayed a depth of empathy that simply could not be taught. Livnat had trained dozens of social workers and concluded that the core skills were innate: students either had them or they didn't. But even the best of them weren't like Huda. She knew how to be genuinely present with patients while also anticipating their every need.

Livnat, who lived in the settlement of Elazar, founded by American Jews, covered her hair with a beret in the modern orthodox style. She admired the way Huda wore her headscarf, which reminded her of her own community. The social work staff called Huda by a Hebraized version of her name: Yehudit Avraham. They saw it as a compliment, an induction.

Livnat worked with another '48 Palestinian, Khalil Khoury, a veteran nurse from Haifa. To him, the hospital felt like one of the only places in Israel where Palestinian citizens seemed somewhat equal to their Jewish coworkers. Although there was plenty of racism in the hospital—Hadassah segregated Arab and Jewish maternity patients at the request of Jewish mothers—Khalil felt well treated by his colleagues. After a patient once told him to go back to Gaza, his Jewish supervisor said the woman was free to go elsewhere. When Ariel Sharon had a stroke in 2005, Khalil helped care for the prime minister and wrote about it in the *American Journal of Nursing*, though he noted that "the presence of Arabs on the [prime minister's] treatment team was considered exceptional." As a '48 Palestinian, Khalil suffered abuse from both sides. PA officials allowed to enter Israel criticized him for paying taxes to the state and working for a Zionist institution. "My parents stayed on the land and you left," Khalil would reply. "And now you're coming here for treatment!"

Khalil and Huda worked with Livnat to compile a list of the missing children. The one that the school provided seemed to be inaccurate. With Khalil and Huda translating, Livnat made her way around the room collecting information—names, identifying features, clothing, photographs—and entering it into a national hospital database. She could use it to check whether the missing children had been registered elsewhere. But nearly all of the victims were in Ramallah, which wasn't linked to the database.

There was pandemonium in the lobby and it spilled into the family center. In most mass casualty events, families would go to the victims' rooms. But there were hardly any victims to go to, just hundreds of relatives, all of them crowded into two small spaces. Livnat saw many more men waiting there than women. She learned that among the families from the West Bank, the men were more likely to have work permits that allowed them to enter Jerusalem. Thinking of her own six children, the youngest close in age to the kindergartners, Livnat suddenly felt for the mothers who were prevented from searching for their little ones.

LATER IN THE day, Livnat was charged with identifying three children who had been transferred from Hadassah Mount Scopus.

The first, a boy named Fadl, had been scorched on his ear and one side of his face; he was soon reunited with his parents. Fadl was in much better shape than the other two: Tala Bahri, whom Eldad Benshtein had brought in his ambulance, and a second boy, still alive but too badly burned to identify.

Livnat couldn't match him to a name or a family. Hours passed and no one came to claim him. Then, toward the end of her shift, two mothers showed up at the hospital looking for their sons. Each had heard there was a boy there who might be hers. At that hour, there were very few children not accounted for. Both women knew that if this boy was not hers, then her own son was most likely dead. It reminded Livnat of the biblical story of the judgment of Solomon, when two mothers came to the king, claiming that the same infant was theirs and that a dead baby belonged to the other woman.

Haya al-Hindi was the first to reach the hospital. Her son Abdullah was one of Tala Bahri's best friends. They sat together in class and always chose one another as partners for school activities. The Hindis lived near the Bahris on the main street of Shuafat Camp, so Tala and Abdullah often rode together on the bus. Haya had spent her whole life in Shuafat Camp; her family had been expelled from Jimzu, a village near Ramle, in 1948. She and her husband, Hafez, lived on the sixth floor of an UNRWA building in the center of the camp. Both had blue IDs. Hafez crossed the checkpoint each morning to work at a pharmacy at a West Jerusalem hospital, Shaare Zedek.

That morning, Haya had prepared her two sons, Abdullah and Ahmad, for the trip. When it was time to leave, Abdullah stayed on the couch, staring at her. She was unnerved by his look. Downstairs, the boys ran into an older cousin, who offered to walk them to the bus in the rain. They left at 7:30 A.M. A little over an hour later, while having breakfast, Haya had to stop eating. She was gripped by a sense of foreboding. Soon after, her phone started buzzing—it was Hafez, wanting to know whether the boys had gone on the trip. Haya dialed Abdullah's teacher, Ula Joulani, but she didn't answer. Haya called her several more times. Then she heard about the accident. She put on an abaya and ran out to the Shuafat checkpoint.

The ride to Ramallah Hospital, eight and a half miles away, took nearly two hours because the traffic was so bad and there were two checkpoints on the way. A man holding a list of names told her that both Ahmad and Abdullah were there. She went searching from room to room, not yet aware of the severity of the accident, not knowing that the bus had flipped and burned. Finally she found Ahmad, sitting naked on a bed. It was cold in the hospital and still raining outside. She looked for a sheet to cover him but couldn't find one. "Why is he naked?" she shouted when she saw a doctor. "Because the children were all burned," he said.

Ahmad's back was bruised but otherwise he was unharmed. He said a man had thrown him out of one of the bus windows. Ahmad recalled that Abdullah wanted them to sit together behind the driver. But Ahmad didn't want to and moved down toward the back. Right after crossing the checkpoint, he said, there had been an earthquake and the bus turned over. All the children and teachers were thrown into a pile. Then there was a fire and little gray bits began to fall on them. Some of the children thought the flakes were snow. A man came into the bus and started lifting the children. Once Ahmad was out of the bus, he didn't see Abdullah again.

Haya searched the rest of the rooms but didn't find Abdullah. A little later, she heard from Hafez's brothers that there was a boy at Hadassah Ein Kerem who might be Abdullah. They all left Ramallah together and got stuck in standstill traffic at the

Qalandia checkpoint, arriving at Ein Kerem long after Hafez. When she got out of the car, she saw what looked like several hundred members of the Hindi clan. They were one of the biggest families in Shuafat Camp.

She was taken to a room where Huda Ibrahim was waiting. Huda explained that a boy had come in; he was in bad shape and Haya would need to give a sample of DNA. A nurse swabbed her mouth. A policewoman then brought her the boy's clothes, some of them badly burned. They were not her son's clothes, Haya said. The policewoman asked her to look again. Haya repeated that she was certain these clothes did not belong to Abdullah. The policewoman insisted: other people had said these were Abdullah's clothes. "You're in shock," she told her.

Haya grew angry. She was being gaslit. Huda stepped in to calm her. "Okay, the boy in the next room isn't yours. You need to go look for your son." The family waited for the DNA results to come back, just to be sure. But then Hafez's brothers were allowed to see the burned boy to confirm that he wasn't Abdullah. They came out crying, but this boy had a mole on his neck. Abdullah was still missing. It was now evening.

NANSY QAWASME AND her mother were called in to see Livnat and Huda, who explained about the boy who had not yet been identified. They asked Nansy for a sample of DNA and to look at the boy's clothes. Most of them had melted into a hard, blackened block, but the edge of a jacket was still discernible. It was Salaah's. Then she saw the teddy bear boxers, which were somehow still whole. Nansy knew now that Salaah was burned, though she had no sense of the extent of it.

Nansy and her mother left the room to wait for the DNA

results, and sat near another mother. It was Haya. As Nansy wept, Haya tried to offer comfort. "I found one of my sons," she said. "I'll find the other one and you'll find yours." Sobbing, Nansy said she had just seen her boy's clothes.

A nurse told Nansy and her family that they were allowed to enter the boy's room. Azzam went first. Nansy's mother watched his face closely as he came out, but he showed no emotion. Azzam's father had been with him and also seemed to have no reaction. Nansy's mother was hopeful: maybe Salaah wasn't in such bad shape. Osama was called in next—and quickly brought out, crying and shouting. As he left the room, he threw up and then fainted. When he came to, he lifted a chair and slammed it against the door and the windows. The staff thought he must be the father. Osama knelt at their mother's feet, weeping and kissing her hands. *"Inshallah khair, inshallah khair."* God willing, it'll be okay. After Nansy's brother Faisal went in, he slammed his fist against the door and broke his hand.

Faisal and Osama begged their mother not to let Nansy go in. "You'll lose your daughter," Osama said. One of the social workers took Nansy's mother aside, telling her there was little left of Salaah. If not for the mole, they wouldn't have been able to identify him. Still, Nansy wanted to see Salaah.

She should wait until after he'd had surgery, the family said, when he'd have new skin. There was a long struggle ahead. She should go home, rest. As they got up to leave the hospital, Nansy saw a doctor who had come out of Salaah's room. She stopped to ask how he was doing. The doctor pointed to the sky: now it is with God.

. . .

Haya left Ein Kerem after 10:00 p.m. There was no point in staying any longer. All the boys there had been accounted for, though Tala Bahri still hadn't been claimed. Tala's father had started his search in the morning, driving from Shuafat Camp to the standstill traffic at the Hizma checkpoint, where he abandoned the car and ran to the accident site. While his sister looked in Ramallah, he caught a ride to Rafidia Hospital in Nablus, then made his way to Ein Kerem. Hours after nightfall, he identified Tala's yellow jacket in an image posted at the family center.

Although there was no news, Haya decided to return to Ramallah Hospital together with Hafez and her family. On the drive there it started to dawn on her that Abdullah must be dead. More than thirteen hours had passed since the accident. Different family members had checked at all the hospitals in Jerusalem. As far as she knew, the only children who had not yet been identified were in the Ramallah morgue. When they got to the hospital, she went directly to the morgue and asked the guard to let her inside. "What do you want to see?" the guard asked. "Charcoal?"

Haya passed out. She woke up in a bed with an IV in her arm and blood dripping from the catheter in her vein. She cursed the hospital, the guard, and the useless staff. She felt a heavy pain in her head, as if her body were absorbing news that her mind refused to accept. The nurses sat her in a wheelchair, and Hafez pushed her down the corridor to visit Ahmad, who was being kept overnight. Before they got to his room, she put her hands on top of her throbbing head and wailed. Hafez should take her home, Haya's mother said. There were plenty of other people to spend the night there with Ahmad.

Haya and Hafez got back to their apartment well after midnight. It was packed with neighbors and family. They checked with the hospital, but the DNA results still weren't in. Haya stayed up all night, watching out the window. There were rumors that some of the children had been taken in by Bedouin in Jaba; maybe a Jaba family would appear in the street below with Abdullah. Before sunrise, Haya did the morning prayer, then changed her clothes and prayed twice more. One of Hafez's brothers came into the kitchen and found her sobbing on the floor. To calm her, he said Abdullah was alive, they had found him. She began to cry even harder. A moment later, the loudspeaker at the mosque announced that Abdullah al-Hindi was dead.

XXIII

On the morning after the accident, Abed and Haifa sat in the kitchen of Abed's mother's place, waiting for news. She had Alzheimer's and no awareness of the crash or that Milad was missing. The DNA results still hadn't come in. Ibrahim came over and called around to his contacts in the PA for updates. He had asked a Jewish friend who lived near Hadassah Ein Kerem to check for Milad there. She called back while Ibrahim was with Abed: Could the parents describe any special physical characteristics? She'd heard there was a boy there with a mole on the front of his neck. Milad did have a mole on his neck, Haifa said, but on the back. The hair color was wrong, too: black, not blond. It's not my son, Abed said.

Visitors came and went until, midmorning, the Salamas received a delegation on behalf of the semitrailer driver, Ashraf Qayqas. Although Ashraf had grown up across the street from Abed, the Qayqas family was not from Anata. They had come after 1967 from a village in the north, Arrabe, near Jenin. It was unusual for a family to move halfway across the West Bank to a small, closely knit town like Anata. Ordinarily people did so only if they needed to escape some sort of trouble. Ashraf's father and his sons had blue Jerusalem IDs, which was suspicious, given that they had not acquired them through marriage and weren't from Jerusalem. It was practically impossible for a family from Jenin to get a blue ID.

People in Anata thought they might be collaborators, which would mean they were under the protection of Israel's security forces. In jail Abed's brother and his cousin Abu Jihad had met prisoners from Arrabe who said that Ashraf's father had fled the village after he was caught informing on a Fatah cell. But the Salamas never brought this up with the Qayqases, and the two families enjoyed respectful relations. Ashraf's family had moved again after Oslo, to Dahiyat a-Salaam, where they could keep their blue IDs, and Ashraf himself married and moved to Beit Safafa, a neighborhood on the Jerusalem side of the wall. It was news to Abed that Ashraf was the driver. In the hours since the accident, he hadn't asked. He didn't care. He knew nothing about the crash itself or who was at fault. Now the delegation from Ashraf's family had come to ask the Salamas for an *atwa*, a temporary truce in tribal law. But Abed had no desire to punish anyone. He had never been the vengeful sort.

Once, Adam had run from the house to escape some children trying to take his toys. He darted into the road in front of a taxi and was sent flying through the air, hitting his head on the ground when he landed. He was hurt, but no bones were broken. Abed's relatives were ready to attack the taxi driver until Abed intervened. The driver was not from Anata. He apologized profusely and wrote his phone number on a piece of paper. Abed told him he didn't want it. "It's my fault," he said. "He's my son and I should have been watching him."

Abed didn't want to think about Ashraf. All he wanted was to find Milad. He granted the *atwa*.

No NEW CHILDREN had been found and it was now midday. The fantasies of Milad appearing at Abed and Haifa's door were fading. In the afternoon, Abed met Bashir back at the Ramallah hospital to wait for the DNA results, leaving Haifa at home with Adam and the girls and a large group of visitors. Then Ibrahim called. He'd managed to get hold of the results through his connections. One of the children in the hospital morgue was Milad.

Although it was afternoon, the sky was already dark, and rain was falling. The Salamas' friends, family, and neighbors began to gather in Anata to receive the body. Adam was outside the house, oblivious to the news, which he soon heard from a cousin. "You're a liar," Adam said. Moments later the announcement came from the mosque's loudspeaker: Milad Salama was dead.

Abed did not want to leave the hospital without seeing his son, but Bashir wouldn't let him. Then Abed said he would ride with Milad to the mosque. Again Bashir stopped him, worried that being alone in the ambulance with Milad would be too much for Abed to bear. So Abed and Bashir drove together, following the ambulance. Bashir thought it was a small mercy that Abed would not see Milad's body before laying him to rest.

Had it been a normal death, Milad would have been brought home to be washed and purified by the men of the family. His left hand would have been placed on his stomach as Abed and his brothers rocked him back and forth until any remaining waste was released. Then he would have been washed three, five, or any odd number of times. Abed and his brothers would have performed *wudu* on Milad's hands and feet, placed cotton in all his orifices, sprayed him with camphor perfume, sprinkled him with powdered henna, and covered him in a white shroud. But none of that could happen now.

Milad was too severely burned for the rituals. In any case the *sulta*, which had announced three days of national mourning, had declared that the dead were martyrs, and martyrs were supposed to be buried in their clothes. Not that Abed cared about *sulta* pronouncements. The hospital had wrapped Milad's body in a white shroud, covered by a brown blanket. He was taken directly to the mosque, in keeping with the custom to bury the dead without delay.

As they entered Anata, Abed saw what must have been thousands of people coming for the funeral. Not just the big families of the town but mourners from all over the West Bank. The women had gathered at Abed's house and other homes, while the men filled the streets on the way to the mosque. Milad's body was carried from the ambulance and placed in a green box. The large crowd of men together recited the prayer for the dead, adding the special supplication for parents mourning the loss of a child. Then another pronouncement from the loudspeaker: Milad Salama would now be buried.

The mass of men walked the short distance from the mosque to the slope of the hillside cemetery, a stone's throw from Abed's house. From the top of the hill, one could see the entire landscape of the accident: over the wall, the villas and playgrounds of Pisgat Ze'ev; beyond them, the IDF Central Command in Neve Yaakov; then the wall running between Neve Yaakov and a-Ram; and, behind a-Ram, the Jaba road, Jaba, and the settlement of Adam.

The funeral and burial happened so quickly Abed never had a moment alone with Milad. The crowd was so large that he couldn't get close to him. Abed was pressed on all sides by friends and family, holding him, pulling at him, preventing him from approaching the grave. His old friend Osama Rajabi, the one who had gone to university in the Soviet Union, stayed by him the whole time. High on the hill, Abed's cousin had built a tomb for his immediate family. Its roof was a rose-colored rectangle of stone tiles, placed perpendicular to the slope, with a row of four small slabs giving access to four still-empty graves. Milad would be buried in the northernmost plot.

Abed's brother Wa'el carried Milad's shrouded body and entered the tomb. In accordance with Islamic law, the body was placed on its side, facing Mecca. Milad's legs were bent at the knees, fixed in the position in which he died, which is how Wa'el left him.

After the burial, Abed was swept along with the crowd of men to the Anata Youth Club, while Haifa and the women of the town remained at home. At the club, where politicians and prominent men gave speeches, Abed got a phone call from someone identifying himself as "Noah," who said he was the head of the Shabak in Anata. "Noah" offered his condolences and Abed thanked him for his words.

ANOTHER CALL CAME the next evening, this time from Palestinian intelligence. A group of angry parents and family were massed at Nour al-Houda threatening to burn the school. Would Abed please go and talk them down? The intelligence officer said he knew Abed didn't blame the school for the crash. He was calling Abed because he was respected in Anata and had moral authority as a bereaved father. The PA forces weren't allowed into Anata, and even if they tried to come, they wouldn't get there in time. Abed agreed.

The crowd outside the school was quite small, and his cousin Abu Jihad and Abu Jihad's brothers seemed to be at the head of it. They were furious that the school had gone ahead with the trip in such a bad storm, that it had used a twenty-seven-year-old bus, which had apparently been in several previous accidents. No one from the school had been in touch to apologize, no one had visited the hospitals or even checked on the injured children.

Abed listened and then spoke. He had lost more than any of them. Yet he still believed Nour al-Houda was a good school, the best in Anata. It was important to the town, not just for the children but the whole community. It provided jobs to dozens of Anata's people. Haifa's sister was a teacher there. Abed was going to keep Adam at the school. "And if Milad came back to me," he said, "I would still send him to Nour al-Houda." Abu Jihad and the others went home.

On THE SECOND day of the *azza*, the three-day mourning period and public wake, Ghazl visited Abed's home. The women's *azza* was held in the salon. The men's mourning hall, at the Anata Youth Club, wouldn't open for several hours, after the midday prayer.

It was the first time Ghazl and Abed had been in the same room since he had come to her office in the education ministry more than fifteen years earlier. She now taught high school science and literature at her alma mater, the Anata girls' school, where she was a much-loved mentor to Abed's two eldest daughters, Lulu and Fufu. Ghazl had come to pay her respects with other women from the school.

Abed hadn't been expecting Ghazl and got up to leave when he saw her, but Haifa urged him to stay. While Ghazl and the teachers offered their condolences to Haifa and her sisters, Abed sat back. He and Ghazl were in the same spot where she had placed his missing necklace in his hand. Although they exchanged no words, the bitterness was gone, trivial in the face of Abed's grief.

After the *azza*, Haifa withdrew into herself. She never talked of the accident and rarely mentioned Milad or spoke his name. For her sake, most people tried to do the same in her presence. Not Abed, though. He refused to be silent, speaking about their son as often as he could bear it. When he did, Haifa would quietly retreat, finding a reason to go to another room. Abed worried for her, wondering when the pain would finally pour out. Perhaps it never would.

XXIV

All Nansy had wanted from Azzam was a hug, some consolation. After leaving the hospital, he went with Nansy to her parents' home in a-Tur, where Sadine was waiting. There, too, he was cold. Later, Nansy couldn't sleep. It had been the longest day of her life and still it wouldn't end. What she was sure was Salaah's Spider-Man backpack appeared and reappeared in images in the news and social media, in photos and videos of the accident. Wide awake, staring at the ceiling, she imagined the crash: where Salaah had sat on the bus, which friend had been next to him, whether he had eaten his candy, what he had done in the moment when the bus flipped over, whether he had called for her.

In the morning she wanted to go back to the hospital. "Go where?" Azzam said. "There's no face, no nose. There's nothing there." Did this man feel anything? How could he have left Salaah's room with such indifference when her brothers had fainted, screamed, broken a hand? At Hadassah, Azzam's mother still wouldn't speak to Nansy. She glared at her as if she were the enemy. Azzam's father said Nansy should look at Salaah. "She sent him on the trip—she should see the result."

So again Nansy asked to go to Salaah. Again her brothers begged her mother to prevent it. Osama held his mother's face and locked eyes with her. "Don't let your daughter do it. She'll go crazy—you'll lose her. If I go to the bathroom, promise me you won't let her go." Again Nansy asked the staff for updates, and the same doctor pointed the same finger toward the sky. She was told that Salaah was heavily sedated and could feel no pain. So she returned to Sadine in a-Tur.

Nansy went back and forth to Hadassah over the next two days. There was no news and still she didn't enter Salaah's room. Her in-laws demanded to know why she hadn't seen him; her family insisted that she absolutely must not. In a-Tur, her parents' neighbors told her Salaah would be okay. They brought food; she barely ate. She was weak, pale, worn down.

In the evening of the third day, Salaah appeared to her in a dream. He was wearing his favorite red coat, which he hadn't taken on the trip, and he was playing with the five dead children. Nansy's mother and aunt also dreamed of Salaah that night. Salaah had spoken to his grandmother. "Tata, I'm going to join my friends," he said, and then walked toward Ula and the five children. Nansy's aunt had dreamed that the prophet Ibrahim had recited the Quran to the dead children and then told them their friend would be joining them.

Nansy felt wholly depleted. She had not been back to the hospital that day. Her family urged her to rest. Her mother told her to pray for the best thing for Salaah, even if it meant death. Before sunset, she felt a pang in her chest, as if someone had squeezed a fist around her heart. Her first thought was that Salaah's soul was leaving his body. She got dressed and told the family she had to see Salaah, now. This time, she said, she would go in the room, look at him with her own eyes. Impatient to leave, she waited in the stairwell and then went down to sit in the car. As her mother was on the way out, she took a call from Azzam's sister, who told her that Salaah had died.

Nansy's mother got in the car, saying nothing to Nansy. They were waiting for her father to finish the sunset prayer at the mosque next door. Exiting the mosque, he answered a call and froze. Nansy saw that something was wrong, but he, too, hid the truth. He said they couldn't go to the hospital because Salaah had caught a bacterial infection. Without the outer protection of skin, burn victims were especially prone to them. They all went back upstairs.

Neighbors followed them into the apartment, and Nansy could tell that there had been a change. Finally, someone said what she already knew. Nansy registered no shock, only remorse. She shouldn't have listened to her family—she should have seen Salaah in the ICU and done right by her son. Compounding Nansy's guilt for signing the permission slip to go on the trip, there was now the deepest regret that she hadn't said goodbye to Salaah.

In the salon, the neighbors said there was a glow around Nansy's face. They swore they had never seen anything like it. The light in the room did seem to have a different quality, just after sunset. But Nansy's mother saw no glow in her daughter's eyes, only anguish.

AZZAM BURIED SALAAH in the same cemetery as Abdullah al-Hindi, in Baab al-Asbaat, next to the Old City walls. For the three days after the funeral, Nansy went to Azzam's family home in Wadi Joz to receive condolences while her in-laws continued to shun her. The few words they directed her way seemed designed to cause torment. "You're his mother. Why didn't you go say goodbye to him?" She heard her father-in-law complaining that she was wearing the same jacket she had on when the accident happened, and it wasn't black.

Nansy couldn't bring herself to return to the apartment in Ras Shehadeh, to Salaah's drawings and toys and clothes. Every inch of the place held a memory of her boy. So she stayed with her parents in a-Tur. People from her neighborhood, from the school, from Anata, asked when she would come to the other side of the wall so they could pay their respects. They hadn't been able to call on her because of their green IDs. Nansy dreaded going back to that walled ghetto.

She was also worried about Sadine. Since the day of the crash, Sadine had started pulling her hair out and scratching her face. For more than a month, she didn't speak. Then Azzam announced that he wanted to take Nansy and Sadine on a trip to Ramallah. It was one of the first humane gestures he had made to his wife. Nansy felt a glimmer of hope. He had been so distant, so cruel. And vicious as well. Days after the funeral, he had forced himself on her.

Nansy was willing to forgive a lot after the accident. She felt pity for Azzam. He, too, was broken and grieving, even if he didn't show it. So the three of them drove toward Ramallah on the Jaba road. Stopping the car on the shoulder, Azzam said this was where the accident had happened. Nansy broke down, sobbing from the pain of his spite. Sadine was in the backseat, watching her mother cry. Nansy wanted to crawl into a hole and die. If Azzam had given her pills or a knife and told her to kill herself, she would have done it there and then. He hadn't meant to hurt her, he said later—he thought she would want to see the site.

At the end of the traditional forty days of mourning, Nansy

learned she was pregnant. Friends and family drew divine meaning from the auspicious date. God had taken her child and was now giving her another one, a better one. How could people be so stupid, she thought. As if there were such a thing as a better one.

The pregnancy put more strain on the marriage. Nansy thought Azzam's family took pleasure in abusing her. "You killed him," her mother-in-law said on several occasions. By the sixth month of her pregnancy, Nansy was frail and exhausted, and spent much of her time in bed replaying memories of her son. When she learned she was carrying a boy, she wanted to name him Salaah. But she had dreams that seemed to warn her against it. In the first, a sheikh handed her a baby whom he called Mohammad. In the second, Salaah brought Nansy a blue onesie, which he said was for his brother Mohammad. So Nansy named the boy Mohammad. He was born on Sadine's fourth birthday, a little more than nine months after Salaah had died.

Then Nansy got pregnant again. She hadn't been trying. In fact, she had been using contraception. Now Azzam wanted a divorce, but first he demanded that she sign away her right to the compensation they collected for Salaah's death. The blue ID holders had received money from Karnit, an Israeli government fund for victims of road accidents; the law specified that anyone hit by an Israeli-owned vehicle had to be paid compensation, no matter where the accident took place, but only if the victims were Israeli or tourists. Green ID holders such as Abed and Haifa would not get a penny from Israel.

Azzam and Nansy had secured slightly more than $200,000. Azzam wanted her to give up not just her share of the money but also everything else: their joint possessions; child support; and the *mahr*, Nansy's dowry in gold.

When Nansy said no, Azzam hit her. He paid a lawyer to draw up a separation agreement and put it in front of her every few days. Each time she refused to sign, he beat her. Sometimes the beatings put her in the hospital. After one incident, she expected a miscarriage. Azzam didn't let up. "Aren't you tired?" he said. "Just sign the papers and you can go." Then he threatened to send her to a mental institution and told her she was losing her mind. He would leave the children's toys in strange places in the apartment and blame it on Nansy. Suspecting him of drugging her, she stopped drinking the coffee he made. He also told her that his sister had pictures of Salaah at the hospital—which was true—and he'd force her to look at them if she wouldn't sign.

Nansy made excuses for him, thinking he had gone mad with grief. Nonetheless, she downloaded a recording app to his phone. What she heard was his sister and father encouraging him to beat her, to do whatever it took to get rid of her. In one recording, his father suggested hiring someone to kill her. Nansy began to fear for her life.

She gave birth to another daughter in March 2014. That summer, when the baby was four months old, Nansy asked her father for money to buy the children presents for Eid al-Fitr. When she came home with bags of new clothes, Azzam was angry and beat her severely. This time Nansy called her brother Osama to come pick her up. Wearing nothing but her nightgown, Nansy took the three children and left Azzam for good.

She moved in with her parents in a-Tur, on the other side of the wall, but their situation remained precarious. Israel had slated the five-story apartment block for demolition. Palestinians were routinely denied permission to build in annexed East Jerusalem—only 13 percent of Palestinian neighborhoods were zoned for construction, and most of that was already developed.

So they were forced to either build illegally or move out. Nansy's parents, like many others, paid hundreds of dollars in fines to the municipality each month, hoping to stave off demolition.

After the divorce, Nansy still wanted Azzam to be a father to his children. He rarely asked to see them, though. Nansy and her parents raised them on their own. The accident had ruined Nansy's life and destroyed her family, but she didn't think she was unusual. It had crushed every family, each in its own way.

Epilogue

A television crew showed up at Abed's door a month after the accident. They were shooting a feature for the weekend news show on Channel 10, one of Israel's main stations. It would air on a Saturday night at the end of March. The title of the segment was "An Arab Kid Died, Ha Ha Ha Ha." The reporter, Arik Weiss, was considered left wing—when he anchored the evening news program some right-wing politicians refused to appear with him.

The hook for the story was not the accident itself but the reaction of young Israelis who had rejoiced at the death of the Palestinian kindergartners. Arik was dismayed by the flood of Facebook posts and online comments celebrating the loss of life: "Hahahaha 10 dead hahahaha, good morning." "It's just a bus full of Palestinians. No big deal. Too bad more didn't die." "Great! Fewer terrorists!!!!" "Joyous news to start the morning." "My day became sweeeeeeeeeeet."

What shocked Arik was not so much the content of the posts but that many of their authors freely paraded their identities. As he said in the voiceover, they wrote "without hiding behind an anonymous keyboard, without shame." And a lot of the posts came from students in middle school and high school. Arik found this puzzling. These teens were living through a period of relative quiet. Some of them were too young to remember the violence of the 1990s and the Second Intifada, yet they seemed to be more racist than older generations. Arik wanted to explore why Israeli youth might feel greater hatred than their elders. He believed the story would hold up a mirror to Israeli society.

At a high school in the coastal town of Hadera, halfway between Haifa and Tel Aviv, Arik interviewed a few of the students who had posted comments under their own names. The segment shows him reading a post to the boy who had written it: "Those little Palestinians could be the terrorist attacks of the future. Don't give me that bullshit that everyone's a human being. They're whores, not people, and they deserve to die." The camera zooms in on the face of the boy, who looks secular and athletic, and is wearing a Hollister T-shirt under an unzipped hoodie.

"You wrote this—" Arik begins to ask.

"—from the heart," the boy says.

He is standing in front of a basketball court while younger preteens are playing behind him. Arik asks whether the boy really meant what he said. "We're talking about four- to five-year-olds, yes?"

"Little kids, so what?"

In the next shot, the boy, now joined by several friends, asks one of them, "Tell me, honestly—you hear about an incident where lots of Palestinian kids are killed. What do you feel, physically? Are you happy, ecstatic?"

"*Walla*," says the friend. "The truth? Ecstatic."

As the camera zooms in on the Facebook comments, Arik's voiceover intones: "It doesn't matter if you're on the left or the right. The fact that someone's celebrating people's death requires us to stop for a moment and ask, How the hell did we get here?"

At another point, the segment shows Abed standing by the side of the road at the site of the accident. In the dirt on the shoulder, someone had placed wooden stakes with pictures of Milad and Salaah. On the drive there, with the camera off, Arik asked Abed in Hebrew if he had seen the jubilant posts. Abed had heard about them. All the parents had. All of Anata and Shuafat Camp had. Most people Abed talked to thought the Israeli authorities had wanted the children to die. Everyone knew how quickly Israeli forces would descend on a West Bank road the moment a kid started throwing stones. Yet the soldiers at the checkpoint, the troops at Rama base, the fire trucks at the settlements nearby, they had all done nothing, letting the bus burn for more than half an hour.

Arik noted that some of the posts came from students in Givat Shaul, the Jerusalem neighborhood that encompasses Deir Yassin, which was the site of the notorious massacre by prestate Jewish paramilitary forces. Abed felt he was being goaded. "We have extremists in our society," he replied. "And you do, too."

THE PROGRAM LATER shows Arik meeting two settlers who live near the accident site. Arik Vaknish is from Adam, where he had moved in 2000. He finished his military service as a guard in Ramallah the same year that Abed was processed in the detention facility there. Like Beber Vanunu, he had grown up in a Moroccan home in Jerusalem and spoke good Arabic. He was a manager at Anglo-Saxon Real Estate, where he sold homes to new Jewish residents in the West Bank.

Together with Beber, Vaknish had worked on the large sign they

posted at the Adam junction after the accident, offering condolences in Hebrew and Arabic. Because of the sign, Channel 10 had
contacted Vaknish and asked him to visit Abed at home in Anata.

The second settler, Duli Yariv from Anatot, had collected
about $1,000 from his neighbors for the grieving families. He,
too, had grown up in Jerusalem, close to Beber and Vaknish's
neighborhood. After finishing his service in the air force, Duli
began to look for a home. He longed for somewhere rural, but his
parents wanted him nearby, and communities inside the Green
Line were too expensive. So he checked out Anatot, which was
beautiful, relatively affordable, and close to family. It was one of
the few places he could build a two-story villa to house his grand
piano and his sister's paintings.

On camera, Duli tells Arik Weiss that he is reluctant to enter
Anata. "It's not a very friendly village, so I wouldn't go in there
by myself without making sure I'm able to get out." The program
shows Vaknish and Duli traveling less than a mile from Anatot
to Anata, passing its graffitied walls, potholed roads, and small
children playing in a street with no sidewalk. "A kilometer and a
half separate the settlement of Anatot from the village of Anata,"
Arik says in voiceover. "Five minutes' drive, a totally different
world." Abed and his brother Wa'el greet the TV crew and the
settlers. The program falsely describes Wa'el as "a suicide bomber"
who was arrested on his way to perpetrate an attack, but correctly
notes that after his release from prison he became a peace activist.
It was through these connections that an Israeli TV crew had
showed up at Abed's door. Abed didn't approve of Wa'el's joint
Israeli-Palestinian activities—what did they achieve, he thought,
besides soothing the Israelis and presenting a false picture of par-
ity between oppressor and oppressed?

Wa'el and Abed sit together on a couch facing Vaknish and

Duli. Yellow drapes block the sunlight in the salon. The Salamas have put out a Styrofoam plate with sweets for their guests. Arik asks Abed if he could bring out pictures of his son. Abed gets up from the couch and returns with a pink album and a large framed photo of Milad. After the Israelis look at the photos, Duli addresses Abed and Wa'el directly. "I want to say to you, I live in Anatot. I'm a settler. When we heard about the accident on the radio, the thought went through my head that the bus was one of ours—and if God had missed by two seconds, it could have been." Duli goes on: "I don't believe anyone from the settlements here in the area could think how great that it's Arab kids. Because tomorrow it'll be our kids." The camera lingers on Abed looking at Duli skeptically.

After Duli and Vaknish leave, the cameraman follows Abed into his bedroom, where he finds a video on his phone. There is Milad in a beanie and winter coat, smiling and laughing as he tells jokes to his father.

Riffing on a saying that a person falling in love will get crushed, Milad begins: "One time, a grain of wheat fell in love and when he came back, he'd been turned into flour."

"Tell another one," says Abed, off camera.

"Another one?" Milad asks.

"Another one."

"About the devil?" Milad suggests. "A man goes into the bathroom," he starts. Instead of the usual prayer to ward off evil, the man whispers the wrong one: "'In the name of God, the most gracious, the most merciful,' the man says, and the devil pisses himself he's laughing so hard!" Milad laughs, and in the video Abed chuckles along with him.

Abed stops watching, covering his face as he begins to weep. The segment ends with that shot.

. . .

ABED'S MOTHER DIED nearly a year after the accident. Alzheimer's had protected her from fully grasping what had happened
to Milad. Within days of her funeral, the Salamas mourned the
loss of another child, an eight-month-old boy who caught a
fatal illness. The baby's father was Ahmad, Abed's cousin who all
those years ago had fought with him and then been attacked in
Makassed Hospital by Na'el wielding a scalpel.

Ahmad was a hard man and stingy as well. He didn't want
to pay for a memorial for his son, so he took over the mourning
hall for Abed's mother. He offered his guests the drinks and dates
Abed's family had put out and he invited visitors for just two days,
rather than the customary three, because that was when the *azza*
for Abed's mother came to an end.

When the time came to bury his son, Ahmad intended to place
him in the same tomb where Milad had been laid to rest. He
didn't want his child's name engraved on a headstone, though,
because of the cost, nor did he want to use an entire plot for the
baby. So he proposed burying him together with Milad.

At first, Abed didn't like the idea. But he came to see it as an
opportunity. He had never had the chance to see Milad or be
alone with him after the accident. He hadn't had a chance to be
alone at all. Some months earlier, he had gone on an organized
hajj to Mecca, and in Medina he had seen Milad's face everywhere he turned—by the columns of the mosque, in the pages
of the Quran, behind the eyes of every young boy he passed. The
group pilgrimage, taken without friends or family, was the closest
he had come to being on his own.

At home, he felt confined and oppressed by everyone around
him: by the crowd at the funeral pulling him away from Milad's

grave, by the relatives surrounding him in his grief, by a society that wouldn't allow a mourning family a single solitary moment, by a culture that insisted a man must always look strong. He wished he could have just an hour to escape, to climb to the top of a mountain and shout. Instead he did his best to hold it in, trying not to shed tears in public.

Suppressing his grief had taken its toll. He developed heart problems and found it hard to walk. He was hospitalized for a blood clot. An echocardiogram indicated "very severe heart failure." The doctor was amazed that Abed was still alive. The truth was he no longer wanted to live. He loved Haifa and Adam and his daughters, but what he longed for most in the world was not possible.

Abed felt he was struggling to accept that his son was really gone. After the television interview, he deleted all his videos of Milad and all but two photos of him. The sight was too painful. He later regretted it. He wanted to see Milad and talk about him, to keep him close, even at the cost of tearing at the wound. If endless grief was the price of holding on to the fading memories of his son, Abed was willing to pay it. It was in the pain of remembering Milad that Abed kept him near.

It was different for Haifa. She still didn't want to speak about Milad. She refused to let the eldest daughter, Lulu, name her child after him. Abed gave up trying to talk about their boy with Haifa. He watched and rewatched a television program about the prophet Yusuf. He saw himself in Yusuf's father, Ya'qub, who would not believe his son was dead. The Quran says that his eyes turned white—he went blind—from his sorrow.

So Abed agreed to Ahmad's request. At the cemetery, Ahmad and his family moved the stone from the entrance to Milad's plot. Before laying their baby to rest, they gave Abed some time alone.

Abed crawled under the stone roof of the tomb and into the very place where his family would eventually bury him. Crouching in the soil beside his son, he could see Milad's body, wrapped in the white shroud in which he had been buried. One day Abed would join him there. He kneeled by the grave for a few minutes. Then at last he said goodbye to Milad.

SOME YEARS LATER, when Abed was working as a taxi driver, he picked up a mother and her children to drive them to Shuafat Camp. As they approached the site of the accident Abed whispered the Fatiha. "May God protect them," the mother said from the backseat. Abed was surprised. "You know about the crash?" he asked. The woman said her son, who was beside her in the taxi, had been there on the bus.

Abed insisted on bringing the family home with him for lunch. They passed Nour al-Houda, where Abed brought Kinder Eggs to Milad's kindergarten classroom each year on the anniversary of the accident. Abed stopped at a store to buy a toy for Milad's old schoolmate. At home, he introduced the boy and his family to Haifa and his daughters. Haifa put her hand on the boy's head and invited the mother and her children to the living room. Sitting on a couch next to the boy, Abed worked up the courage to ask him if he remembered anything about Milad that day. "Milad was in the front of the bus," the boy said. "He was scared and he crawled under his seat."

After Anata's memories of the crash faded, Abed and Haifa shut themselves in. People in the town barely saw them. As the seventh anniversary approached, Abed saw a Facebook post by Milad's seventeen-year-old cousin Rama. Though they had attended the same school, Rama was five years older than Milad.

Abed didn't think they had been close, but Rama wrote about Milad with affection, and noted the upcoming date. Abed went to Rama's home to ask why, all these years later, she had thought to post about his son. "I was the last one to kiss him," she said. "Before Milad got on the bus, he gave me a chocolate egg, and I kissed him on the cheek."

ASHRAF QAYQAS WAS sentenced to thirty months in prison, a remarkably lenient punishment for an act of gross negligence that killed seven people. He developed leukemia during the trial, and his defense attorney, a '48 Palestinian from Acre, believed that the cancer was the reason for the light sentence. When Ashraf appealed the conviction, Israel's Supreme Court denied his petition. "Every person is a world and its entirety," wrote Justice Neal Hendel in his ruling. "The death of seven people is a disaster that cannot be measured by simple multiplication. The loss is greater than the sum of its parts."

The trial and police investigation focused narrowly on the actions of the driver, ignoring the broader causes of the accident, of the fatalities, and of the woefully late emergency response. Some of the Israeli ambulances coming from Jerusalem had been delayed by the army, waiting for it to open a gate in the separation wall at the Qalandia checkpoint. The emergency services coming from West Bank settlements or through the Hizma checkpoint had also been delayed, in their case by dispatchers sending them to the wrong place, to the Adam roundabout. Israelis commonly referred to areas of the West Bank by the names of the nearest settlement, since most weren't familiar with the Palestinian roads and villages.

Other emergency responders told Israeli media that it took

them "quite some time to find the exact location because it is Palestinian territory." But the Jaba road was not in PA territory. While it served hundreds of thousands of Palestinians, the road was under full Israeli control.

Days after the accident, the PA formed a ministerial committee to investigate the causes. Its report noted that "the nearest Israeli ambulance, emergency services, and fire station are only a minute and a half away," while sending "Palestinian ambulances and emergency vehicles" to the Jaba road "requires coordination with Israel." Also, Palestinian emergency services were impeded by the "suffocating traffic" at the Qalandia and Jaba checkpoints, and previous Palestinian requests to install lighting and a central divider in the road had been "rejected by Israel." In sum, this placed the "moral and legal responsibility on the Israeli side." The bereaved parents dismissed the report as shoddy, rushed, and inaccurate, aimed at covering up the PA's own inadequate rescue and its negligent oversight of the schools and their safety.

For all the blame that was cast, no one—not the investigators, not the lawyers, not the judges—named the true origins of the calamity. No one mentioned the chronic lack of classrooms in East Jerusalem, a shortage that led parents to send their children to poorly supervised West Bank schools. No one pointed to the separation wall and the permit system that forced a kindergarten class to take a long, dangerous detour to the edge of Ramallah rather than driving to the playgrounds of Pisgat Ze'ev, a stone's throw away.

There was no suggestion that Israel's fund for accident victims should compensate the families of green ID holders, whose children were killed on a road controlled by Israel and patrolled by its police. No one argued that a single, badly maintained artery was insufficient for the north-south transit of Palestinians in the greater Jerusalem–Ramallah area, or objected that the checkpoints were used to stem Palestinian movement and ease settler traffic at rush hour. No one noted that the absence of emergency services on one side of the separation wall was bound to lead to tragedy. No one said that the Palestinians in the area were neglected because the Jewish state aimed to reduce their presence in greater Jerusalem, the place most coveted by Israel. For these acts, no one was held to account.

AUTHOR'S NOTE

This is a work of nonfiction. All of the names in the book are real, except for those of four people—Abu Hassan, Azzam, Ghazl, and Hassan—out of respect for their privacy.

I chose not to use a single standard for Arabic and Hebrew transliterations. Too many of the words already have commonly accepted English transliterations, which I used where possible, even though they are highly inconsistent. For words that are not as widely known in English, I transliterated in a way that I hope will balance ease of reading with accuracy of pronunciation for readers unfamiliar with the languages.

Currencies converted to US dollars have been adjusted for inflation and presented in June 2023 amounts.

SOURCES

EPIGRAPH

Cavell, Stanley. *The Senses of Walden: An Expanded Edition.* Chicago: University of Chicago Press, 1992.

PROLOGUE

Author interviews with Dror Etkes, Abed Salama, Adam Salama, Haifa Salama, and Mohammad (Abu Wisaam) Salama.

Altman, Yair. "Truck, Bus Collide in Jerusalem; 8 Dead." *Ynet* [Hebrew], 16 February 2012.

Applied Research Institute—Jerusalem. "Jericho City Profile." 2012.

Etkes, Dror. "Anata." Unpublished paper, 2015.

Israeli Civil Administration for Judea and Samaria. "Arcgis—Information for the Public" [Hebrew]. Accessed 26 July 2022.

Ma'an Development Center. "Anata: Confinement to a Semi Enclave." December 2007.

Palestinian Central Bureau of Statistics. "Jerusalem Statistical Yearbook No. 12" [Arabic]. June 2010.

Seitz, Charmaine. "Jerusalem's Anata Out of Options." *Jerusalem Quarterly*, no. 32, Autumn 2007.

Thrall, Nathan. "A Day in the Life of Abed Salama." *New York Review of Books* (online), 19 March 2021.

PART ONE | THREE WEDDINGS

Author interviews with Dror Etkes, Abed Salama, Bashir Salama, Haifa Salama, Ibrahim Salama, Mohammad (Abu Wisaam) Salama, Naheel Salama, Wa'el Salama.

Adalah. "The October 2000 Killings." 11 August 2020.

American Friends Service Committee. "Palestine Refugee Relief, Bulletin No. 1." March 1949.

Amnesty International. "50 Years of Israeli Occupation: Four Outrageous Facts About Military Order 101." 25 August 2017.

———. "1990 Report." 1990, 129–32.

Applied Research Institute—Jerusalem. "Anata Town Profile." 2012.

Beinin, Joel, and Lisa Hajjar. "Palestine, Israel and the Arab-Israeli Conflict: A Primer." Middle East Research and Information Project, 2014.

Blankfort, Jeffrey. "Massacre at Rishon Lezion: Killer of Gaza." *Middle East Labor Bulletin* 2, no. 3, Summer 1990.

B'Tselem, "Acting the Landlord: Israel's Policy in Area C, the West Bank." June 2013.

———. "Banned Books and Authors, Information Sheet." 1 October 1989.

———. "Detained Without Trial: Administrative Detention in the Occupied Territories Since the Beginning of the Intifada." October 1992.

———. "Fatalities in the first Intifada." Accessed 12 November 2022.

———. "Freedom of Movement." 11 November 2017.

———. "Information Sheet." 1 August 1989.

———. "Statistics on Revocation of Residency in East Jerusalem." 7 April 2021.

———. "Statistics on Settlements and Settler Population." Accessed 26 July 2022.

Canada: Immigration and Refugee Board of Canada. "Palestine: Whether a Palestinian Formerly Residing in East Jerusalem Who Had His Israeli Identity Card Revoked Is Able to Live in the West Bank or the Gaza Strip." 1 February 1999.

———. "Palestine: Whether a Permit Is Required from Israel for a Palestinian Resident of Bethlehem to Travel to Work in Ramallah and Back, Whether a Permit Guarantees Free Movement Past Checkpoints." 4 July 2001.

Chatty, Dawn, and Gillian Lewando Hundt, editors. *Children of Palestine: Experiencing Forced Migration in the Middle East.* New York: Berghahn Books, 2005.

Ciotti, Paul. "Israeli Roots, Palestinian Clients: Taking the Arab Cause to Court Has Earned Jewish Lawyer Lea Tsemel the Wrath of Her Countrymen." *Los Angeles Times*, 27 April 1988.

Foundation for Middle East Peace. "Comprehensive Settlement Population 1972–2011." 13 January 2012.

Government of Israel. "Commission of Inquiry into the Clashes Between Security Forces and Israeli Citizens in October 2000." August 2003.

———. "The Counter-Terrorism Law, 5776–2016." 2016.

———. "Prevention of Terrorism Ordinance No 33, 5708–1948." 1948.

Hammami, Rema. "Women, the Hijab and the Intifada." *Middle East Report*, May/June 1990, 164–65.

Hass, Amira. "Israel's Closure Policy: An Ineffective Strategy of Containment and Repression." *Journal of Palestine Studies* 31, no. 3, Spring 2002, 5–20.

Hiltermann, Joost R. *Behind the Intifada: Labor and Women's Movements in the Occupied Territories*. Princeton: Princeton University Press, 1991.

———. "Trade Unions and Women's Committees: Sustaining Movement, Creating Space." *Middle East Report*, no. 164/165, May-August 1990, 32–53.

Hiroyuki, Suzuki. "Understanding the Palestinian Intifada of 1987: Historical Development of the Political Activities in the Occupied Territories." *Annals of Japan Association for Middle East Studies* 29, no. 2, 171–97.

Hoffman, David. "The Intifada's Lost Generation." *Washington Post*, 7 December 1992.

———. "Palestinians Reconsider Their Tactics." *Washington Post*, 27 June 1993.

Human Rights Watch. "Justice Undermined: Balancing Security and Human Rights in the Palestinian Justice System." 13, no. 4 (E), November 2001.

———. "Prison Conditions in Israel and the Occupied Territories." April 1991.

Inbar, Efraim. "Israel's Small War: The Military Response to the Intifada." *Armed Forces & Society* 18, no. 1, 1991, 29–50.

Israeli Central Bureau of Statistics. "Statistical Abstract of Israel, 1992–2008." 2009.

Israel Defense Forces. "Order No. 101: Order Regarding Prohibition of Incitement and Hostile Propaganda Actions" [Hebrew]. 22 August 1967.

Jerusalem Institute for Israel Studies. "Statistical Yearbook of Jerusalem, 1991–2008." 2009.

Johnson, Penny, and Rema Hammami. "Change & Conservation: Family Law Reform in Court Practice and Public Perceptions in the Occupied Palestinian Territory." Institute of Women's Studies, Birzeit University, December 2013.

Landau, Efi. "Ilan Biran: Barak, Ben-Eliezer Promised to Privatize Bezeq Within Year." *Globes*, 26 September 1999.

Lesch, Ann M. "Prelude to the Uprising in the Gaza Strip." *Journal of Palestine Studies* 20, no. 1. Autumn 1990, 1–23.

Lieber, Dov. "In the Heart of Jerusalem, a Squalid Palestinian 'Refugee Camp' Festers." *Times of Israel*, 26 December 2016.

Lybarger, Loren D. *Identity and Religion in Palestine: The Struggle Between Islamism and Secularism in the Occupied Territories.* Princeton: Princeton University Press, 2007.

Ma'oz, Moshe. *Palestinian Leadership on the West Bank: The Changing Role of the Arab Mayors Under Jordan and Israel.* New York: Routledge, 1984.

Neff, Donald. "The Intifada Erupts, Forcing Israel to Recognize Palestinians." *Washington Report on Middle East Affairs*, December 1997, 81–83.

Norwegian Refugee Council. "Undocumented and Stateless: The Palestinian Population Registry and Access to Residency and Identity Documents in the Gaza Strip." January 2012.

Oren, Aya. "The Indictment Against Ami Popper: Murdered Seven and Tried to Murder Ten." *Ma'ariv* [Hebrew], 19 June 1990.

Palestinian Central Bureau of Statistics. "Jerusalem Statistical Yearbook," no. 12 [Arabic], June 2010.

Pedatzur, Reuven. "More Than a Million Bullets." *Haaretz*, 29 June 2004.

Peretz, Don. "Intifadeh: The Palestinian Uprising." *Foreign Affairs*, Summer 1988.

Reuters. "Israeli Acquitted in Traffic Mishap That Sparked Arab Riots." 7 March 1992.

Rinat, Zafrir. "Jews Have a Discount, Arabs the Full Price." *Haaretz* [Hebrew], 26 July 2013.

Sofer, Roni. "The Indictment Against the Driver Who Is Considered One of the Causes of the Intifada." *Ma'ariv* [Hebrew], 6 December 1989.

Tzaitlin, Uriel. "30 Years: This Is the Story of the Intifada." *Kol Hazman* [Hebrew], 15 December 2017.

United Nations Division for Palestinian Rights. "Chronological Review of Events Relating to the Question of Palestine—October 2000." 31 October 2000.

United States Department of State. "Country Reports on Human Rights Practices for 1984: Report Submitted to the Committee on Foreign Relations, U.S. Senate, and Committee on Foreign Affairs, U.S. House of Representatives," 1260–268.

———. "Key Officers of Foreign Service Posts: Guide for Business Representatives." September 1990.

United States Embassy in Israel. "History of the U.S. Diplomatic Presence in Jerusalem & of Our Agron Road Location." Accessed 26 July 2022.

Usher, Graham. *Dispatches from Palestine: The Rise and Fall of the Oslo Peace Process.* London: Pluto Press, 1999.

Yesh Din and Emek Shaveh. "Appropriating the Past: Israel's Archaeological Practices in the West Bank." December 2017.

Zureik, Elia, David Lyon, and Yasmeen Abu-Laban, editors. *Surveillance and Control in Israel/Palestine: Population, Territory, and Power.* New York: Routledge, 2011.

PART TWO | TWO FIRES

Author interviews with Salem Abu Markhiye, Milena Ansari, Huda Dahbour, Ashraf Joulani, Imm Ashraf Joulani, Mohannad Joulani, Saadi (Abu Ashraf) Joulani, Saadi Joulani, Mira Lapidot, Yaakov Lapidot, Mansour Nasasra, Rita Qahwaji.

Abdul Jawwad, Saleh. "The Classification and Recruitment of Collaborators." In *The Phenomenon of Collaboration in Palestine.* Jerusalem: PASSIA, 2001.

Abu Ras, Thabet. "The Arab-Bedouin Population in the Negev: Transformations in an Era of Urbanization." The Abraham Fund Initiatives. March 2012.

Adalah. "Bedouin Citizens of Israel in the Naqab (Negev): A Primer." 2019.

Al-Haq. "Waiting for Justice—Al-Haq: 25 Years Defending Human Rights (1979–2004)." June 2005.

Ali, Ahmed. *Al-Qur'an: A Contemporary Translation.* Princeton: Princeton University Press, 2001.

Aloni, Shlomo. *Israeli F-15 Eagle Units in Combat.* Oxford: Osprey Publishing, 2006.

Angrist, Joshua. "The Palestinian Labor Market Between the Gulf War and Autonomy." MIT Department of Economics, Working Paper. May 1998.

Applied Research Institute—Jerusalem. "Abu Dis Town Profile." 2012.

————. "As Sawahira ash Sharqiya Town Profile." 2012.

Bergman, Ronen. *Rise and Kill First: The Secret History of Israel's Targeted Assassinations.* New York: Random House, 2018.

Bimkom. "The Bedouin Communities East of Jerusalem—A Planning Survey." Accessed 26 July 2022.

————. "Survey of Palestinian Neighborhoods in East Jerusalem: Planning Problems and Opportunities." 2013.

B'Tselem. "Collaborators in the Occupied Territories: Human Rights Abuses and Violations." 1994.

————. "The Military Courts." 11 November 2017.

————. "No Minor Matter: Violation of the Rights of Palestinian Minors Arrested by Israel on Suspicion of Stone Throwing." July 2011.

————. "Palestinian Minors Killed by Israeli Security Forces in the West Bank, Before Operation 'Cast Lead.'" B'Tselem website. Accessed 26 July 2022.

————. "Statistics: Palestinians Killed by Israeli Security Forces in the West Bank, Before Operation 'Cast Lead.'" B'Tselem website. Accessed 26 July 2022.

B'Tselem and HaMoked. "Forbidden Families Family Unification and Child Registration in East Jerusalem." January 2004.

Cook, Jonathan. "Bedouin in the Negev Face New 'Transfer.'" *Middle East Report Online*, 10 May 2003.

Dahbour, Ahmad. *Diwan* [Arabic]. Beirut: Dar al-'Awdah, 1983.

————. *Huna, Hunak* [Arabic]. Amman: Dar al-Shurouq, 1997, translated by Khaled Furani in Khaled Furani, *Silencing the Sea: Secular Rhythms in Palestinian Poetry.* Stanford: Stanford University Press, 2012.

————. "We Died for Kufr Kanna to Live." In Kawther Rahmani, "A Portrait of the Late Palestinian Poet Ahmad Dahbour," *Shafaqna*, 25 May 2017.

Defense for Children International-Palestine. "No Way to Treat a Child, Palestinian Children in the Israeli Military Detention System." April 2016.

Druckman, Yaron. "99.7% of Palestinians Are Convicted in Military Courts." *Ynet* [Hebrew], 6 January 2008.

Dunstan, Simon. *The Yom Kippur War 1973 (1): The Golan Heights.* Oxford: Osprey Publishing, 2003.

Falah, Ghazi. "How Israel Controls the Bedouin in Israel." *Journal of Palestine Studies* 14, no. 2, Winter 1985, 35–51.

Furani, Khaled. *Silencing the Sea: Secular Rhythms in Palestinian Poetry.* Stanford: Stanford University Press, 2012.

GISHA. "A Guide to the Gaza Closure: In Israel's Own Words." September 2011.

HaMoked. "Temporary Order? Life in East Jerusalem Under the Shadow of the Citizenship and Entry into Israel Law." September 2014.

Human Rights Watch. "Children Behind Bars: The Global Overuse of Detention of Children." 2016.

———. "Stateless Again: Palestinian-Origin Jordanians Deprived of Their Nationality." 1 February 2010.

Israeli Air Force. "The Long Leg." Accessed 26 July 2022.

———. "Operation 'Wooden Leg.'" Accessed 26 July 2022.

Israeli Ministry of Foreign Affairs. "Address to the Knesset by Prime Minister Rabin on the Israel-Palestinian Interim Agreement." 5 October 1995. Accessed October 1, 2016.

JTA Staff. "Arafat Cries After Learning Rabin Is Dead." *Jewish Telegraphic Agency*, 10 November 1995.

Khalidi, Walid. "The Fall of Haifa Revisited." *Journal of Palestine Studies* 37, no. 3, Spring 2008.

Kimmerling, Baruch, and Joel S. Migdal. *The Palestinian People: A History.* Cambridge: Harvard University Press, 2003.

al-Labadi, Dr. Abdel Aziz. *My Story with Tel al-Za'atar* [Arabic]. Beirut: Editions Difaf, 2016.

Labidi, Arwa. "October 1, 1985. The Day the Israeli Occupation Army Bombed Tunisia." *Inkyfada*, 1 October 2021.

Levinson, Chaim. "Nearly 100% of All Military Court Cases in West Bank End in Conviction, Haaretz Learns." *Haaretz*, 29 November 2011.

Middle East Research and Information Project. "Why Syria Invaded Lebanon." *MERIP Reports*, no. 51, October 1976, 3–10.

Morris, Benny. *The Birth of the Palestinian Refugee Problem Revisited.* Cambridge: Cambridge University Press, 2004.

———. *Israel's Border Wars, 1949–1956.* Oxford: Oxford University Press, 1993.

———. *1948: A History of the First Arab-Israeli War.* New Haven: Yale University Press, 2009.

Nasasra, Mansour. *The Naqab Bedouins: A Century of Politics and Resistance.* New York: Columbia University Press, 2017.

———. "Two Decades of Bedouin Resistance and Survival Under Israeli Military Rule, 1948–1967." *Middle Eastern Studies* 56, no. 1, 2020, 64–83.

al-Osta, Adel. "A Family Is Looking for Their Children . . . Maryam al-'Asra.'" *Romman* [Arabic], 6 June 2017.

Palestinian Central Bureau of Statistics. "Estimated Population in Palestine Mid-Year by Governorate,1997–2021." Accessed 26 July 2022.

———. "Press Release on the Occasion of Palestinian Prisoners Day: More Than 650,000 Palestinian Were Exposed to Detention Since 1967, of Whom 9,400 Are Still in Prison." 17 April 2006.

Palmer, E. H. *The Survey of Western Palestine: Arabic and English Name Lists.* London: The Committee of the Palestine Exploration Fund. 1881.

Parsons, Nigel. *The Politics of the Palestinian Authority: From Oslo to al-Aqsa.* New York: Routledge, 2005.

Prial, Frank J. "Israeli Planes Attack P.L.O. in Tunis, Killing at Least 30; Raid 'Legitimate,' U.S. Says." *New York Times,* 2 October 1985.

Rees, Matt. "Untangling Jenin's Tale." *Time,* 13 May 2002.

Reilly, James A. "Israel in Lebanon, 1975–1982." *Middle East Report,* no. 108, September/October 1982.

Rothschild, Walter. "Arthur Kirby and the Last Years of Palestine Railways: 1945–1948." Doctoral thesis presented to King's College, London, December 2007.

Sayigh, Yezid. *Armed Struggle and the Search for State: The Palestinian National Movement, 1949–1993.* New York: Oxford University Press, 1999.

Shulman, David. "The Bedouins of al-Khan al-Ahmar Halt the Bulldozers of Israel." *New York Review of Books* (online), 26 October 2018.

Smith, William E. "Israel's 1,500-Mile Raid." *Time,* 14 October 1985.

Suwaed, Muhammad Youssef. "Bedouin-Jewish Relations in the Negev 1943–1948." *Middle Eastern Studies* 51, no. 5, 2015, 767–88.

Tarazi, Monica. "Planning Apartheid in the Naqab." *Middle East Report,* no. 253, Winter 2009.

Tartir, Alaa. "The Evolution and Reform of Palestinian Security Forces 1993–2013." *Stability: International Journal of Security and Development* 4, no. 1, 2015.

Thrall, Nathan. *The Only Language They Understand: Forcing Compromise in Israel and Palestine.* New York: Metropolitan Books, 2017.

United Nations Division for Palestinian Rights. "Chronological Review of Events Relating to the Question of Palestine." May 2004.

United Nations Human Rights Council. "Report of the Special Rappor-
teur on the Situation of Human Rights in the Palestinian Territories
Occupied Since 1967, John Dugard." 21 January 2008.
United Nations Office for the Coordination of Humanitarian Affairs. "The
Impact of Israel's Separation Barrier on Affected West Bank Commu-
nities." March 2004.
———. "Protection of Civilians Weekly Report." 3–9 August 2011.
United Nations Office of the Special Coordinator in the Occupied Terri-
tories. "Economic and Social Conditions in the West Bank and Gaza
Strip." 15 April 1998.
United Nations Relief and Works Agency. "Fifteenth Progress Report
Covering March and April 2002." 2002.
———. "Profile: Abu Dis, East Jerusalem." March 2004.
United Nations Special Committee on Palestine. "Report to the General
Assembly." Official Records of the Second Session of the General
Assembly, Supplement no. 11, 3 September 1947.
Warren, Col. Sir Charles, and Capt. Claude Reigner Conder. *The Survey of
Western Palestine: Jerusalem.* London: The Committee of the Palestine
Exploration Fund, 1884.

PART THREE | MASS CASUALTY INCIDENT

Author interviews with Salem Abu Markhiye, Dvir Adani, Amnon Amir,
Ghadeer Bahri, Ibrahim Bahri, Imm Mohammad Bahri, Mohammad
Bahri, Muhannad Bahri, Rula Bahri, Tala Bahri, Eldad Benshtein, Itzhak
Bloch, Itai Elias, Raphael Herbst, Namir Idilby, Wadah Khatib, Nadav
Matzner, Nader Morrar, Bentzi Oiring, Ilay Peled, Shlomo Petrover, Ami
Shoshani, Fathiya Tawam, Mustafa Tawam, Nageebeh Tawam, Saar Tzur,
Arik Vaknish, Beber Vanunu, Dubi Weissenstern, Maysoon Zahalka.
Altman, Yair. "8 Dead When a Children's Bus Overturned Near Jerusalem."
Ynet [Hebrew], 16 February 2012.
Applied Research Institute—Jerusalem. "Beit Duqqu Village Profile." 2012.
———. "Jaba Village Profile." 2012.
———. "Tuqu Town Profile." 2010.
Breiner, Josh. "Prominent Haredi Rescue Organization Inflated Data, and
Received Millions of Shekels as a Result." *Haaretz*, 18 December 2022.
B'Tselem. "Statistics on Settlements and Settler Population." Accessed 26
July 2022.
Emek Shaveh. "On Which Side Is the Grass Greener? National Parks in
Israel and the West Bank." December 2017.

Goldberg, Haim. "19 Years Later: Bentzi Oiring Celebrated the Engagement of the Baby He Saved." *Kikar Hashabbat* [Hebrew], 4 February 2021.

Israeli Central Bureau of Statistics. "Table 2.53: Immigrants, by Period of Immigration and Last Continent of Residence." 13 October 2021.

Israeli Civil Administration for Judea and Samaria. "Arcgis—Information for the Public." Accessed 26 July 2022.

Israeli Police. "Testimony of Ashraf Qayqas Before Police Officer Shmuel Ozeri" [Hebrew]. 16 February 2012.

Israeli Police, Shai (Shomron-Yehuda) District, Traffic Division. "Expert Opinion: Analysis of the Tachnograph Disc" [Hebrew]. 28 February 2012.

———. "Incident Report" [Hebrew]. 2012.

———. "Presentation of the Results of the Examination of the Vericom" [Hebrew]. 10 April 2012.

———. "Testimony of Ashraf Qayqas Before Traffic Investigator Eliyahu Mizrahi" [Hebrew]. 21 February 2012.

———. "Traffic Examiner Report" [Hebrew]. 8 May 2012.

Jerusalem District Court. "The State of Israel v. Ashraf Qayqas: Hearing on 29 March 2015" [Hebrew], 29 March 2015, 25–136.

———. "The State of Israel v. Ashraf Qayqas: Hearing on 16 June 2015" [Hebrew], 16 June 2015, 26–120.

———. The State of Israel v. Ashraf Qayqas: Hearing on 9 June 2016" [Hebrew], 9 June 2016, 29–91.

———. "The State of Israel v. Ashraf Qayqas: Hearing on 14 June 2016" [Hebrew], 14 June 2016, 28–99.

———. "The State of Israel v. Ashraf Qayqas: Hearing on 15 June 2016" [Hebrew], 15 June 2016, 28–74.

———. "The State of Israel v. Ashraf Qayqas: Hearing on 23 March 2017" [Hebrew], 23 March 2017, 32–92.

———. "The State of Israel v. Ashraf Qayqas: Sentence" [Hebrew], 29 March 2018, 1–17.

Palestinian Authority Government. "The Full Report of the Ministerial Committee in Charge of Investigating the Traffic Accident in Jaba." *Wafa* [Arabic], 18 March 2012.

Palestinian Central Bureau of Statistics. "Localities in Jerusalem Governorate by Type of Locality and Population Estimates, 2007–2016." Accessed 26 July 2022.

Solomon, Zahava, and Rony Berger. "Coping with the Aftermath of Terror-Resilience of ZAKA Body Handlers." *Journal of Aggression, Maltreatment & Trauma* 10, no. 1–2, 2005, 593–604.

Union of Fire and Rescue Services in Judea and Samaria and the Jordan
    Valley. "Investigation of the Burning of the Children's Bus." 22 February
    2012.
ZAKA. "ZAKA Again in the Top Three" [Hebrew]. 28 November 2016.

PART FOUR | THE WALL

Author interviews with Ghadeer Bahri, Ibrahim Bahri, Mohammad Bahri,
    Rula Bahri, Abed Salama, Ibrahim Salama, Ron Shatzberg, Yehuda
    Shaul, Adi Shpeter, Dany Tirza, Saar Tzur, Arik Vaknish, Beber Vanunu.
Akevot. "Erasure of the Green Line." June 2022.
Almog, Shmuel. "Between Zionism and Antisemitism." *Patterns of Prejudice*
    28, no. 2, 1994, 49–59.
———. "'Judaism as Illness': Antisemitic Stereotype and Self-Image."
    History of European Ideas 13, no. 6, 1991, 793–804.
Alroey, Gur. "Two Historiographies: Israeli Historiography and the Mass
    Jewish Migration to the United States, 1881–1914." *The Jewish
    Quarterly Review* 105, no. 1, Winter 2015, 99–129.
Aly, Götz. *Europe Against the Jews, 1880–1945.* New York: Metropolitan
    Books, 2020.
Aran, Amnon. *Israeli Foreign Policy Since the End of the Cold War.* Cam-
    bridge: Cambridge University Press, 2021.
Arens, Moshe. "Tear Down This Wall." *Haaretz,* 5 March 2013.
Arieli, Shaul. "Messianism Meets Reality: The Israeli Settlement Project in
    Judea and Samaria: Vision or Illusion, 1967–2016." Economic Coop-
    eration Foundation, November 2017.
Arieli, Shaul, and Doubi Schwartz, with the participation of Hadas Tagari.
    "Injustice and Folly: On the Proposals to Cede Arab Localities from
    Israel to Palestine." The Floersheimer Institute for Policy Studies, Pub-
    lication no. 3/48e, July 2006.
Associated Press Staff. "Middle East—Reactions to Hebron Agreement."
    Associated Press, 15 January 1997.
Backmann, René. *A Wall in Palestine.* New York: Picador, 2010.
Barkan, Noam. "The Secret Story of Israel's Transit Camps." *Ynet* [Hebrew],
    3 March 2019.
Baumann, Hanna, and Manal Massalha. "'Your Daily Reality Is Rubbish':
    Waste as a Means of Urban Exclusion in the Suspended Spaces of East
    Jerusalem." *Urban Studies* 59, no. 3, 2022, 548–71.
Ben-Gurion, David. *Memoirs, David Ben-Gurion.* New York: World Pub-
    lishing Company, 1970.

Bimkom. "Survey of Palestinian Neighborhoods in East Jerusalem: Planning Problems and Opportunities." 2013.

Bishara, Azmi. "On the Question of the Palestinian Minority in Israel." *Theory and Criticism* [Hebrew] 3, 1993, 7–20.

Bloom, Etan. "What 'The Father' Had in Mind? Arthur Ruppin (1876–1943), Cultural Identity, Weltanschauung and Action." *History of European Ideas* 33, no. 3, September 2007, 330–49.

Bradley, Megan. *Refugee Repatriation: Justice, Responsibility and Redress.* Cambridge: Cambridge University Press, 2013.

B'Tselem. "Arrested Development: The Long Term Impact of Israel's Separation Barrier in the West Bank." October 2012.

———. "Behind the Barrier: Human Rights Violations as a Result of Israel's Separation Barrier." March 2003.

———. "Impossible Coexistence: Human Rights in Hebron Since the Massacre at the Cave of the Patriarchs." September 1995.

———. "Judgment of the High Court of Justice in Beit Sourik." 1 January 2011.

———. "Playing the Security Card: Israeli Policy in Hebron as a Means to Effect Forcible Transfer of Local Palestinians." September 2019.

———. "Statistics: Israeli Civilians Killed by Palestinians in the West Bank, Before Operation Cast Lead." B'Tselem website. Accessed 26 July 2022.

———. "Statistics: Israeli Civilians Killed by Palestinians in the West Bank, Since Operation Cast Lead." B'Tselem website. Accessed 26 July 2022.

———. "Statistics: Israeli Security Force Personnel Killed by Palestinians in the West Bank, Before Operation Cast Lead." B'Tselem website. Accessed 26 July 2022.

———. "Statistics: Israeli Security Force Personnel Killed by Palestinians in the West Bank, Since Operation Cast Lead." B'Tselem website. Accessed 26 July 2022.

Cattan, Henry. "The Question of Jerusalem." *Arab Studies Quarterly* 7, no. 2/3, Spring/Summer 1985, 131–60.

Davis, Uri. *Apartheid Israel: Possibilities for the Struggle Within.* New York: Zed Books, 2003.

Dekel, Udi, and Lia Moran-Gilad. "The Annapolis Process: A Missed Opportunity for a Two-State Solution?" INSS. June 2021.

Doron, Joachim. "Classic Zionism and Modern Anti-Semitism: Parallels and Influences (1883–1914)." *Studies in Zionism* 4, no. 2, 2008, 169–204.

Dumper, Michael. "Policing Divided Cities: Stabilization and Law Enforcement in Palestinian East Jerusalem." *International Affairs* 89, no. 5, 2013, 1247–64.

Economic Cooperation Foundation. "Summary of a Meeting Between the Head of the Tanzim in Anata and the Representative of the Anatot Settlement" [Hebrew], 9 November 2000.

Eitan, Uri, and Aviv Tatarsky, Oshrat Maimon, Ronit Sela, Nisreen Alyan, Keren Tzafrir. "The Failing East Jerusalem Education System." Ir Amim and the Association for Civil Rights in Israel, August 2013.

Eldar, Akiva. "Sharon's Bantustans Are Far from Copenhagen's Hope." *Haaretz*, 13 May 2003.

Enderlin, Charles. *Shattered Dreams: The Failure of the Peace Process in the Middle East, 1995–2002.* New York: Other Press, 2003.

Ephron, Dan. *Killing a King: The Assassination of Yitzhak Rabin and the Remaking of Israel.* New York: W. W. Norton & Company, 2015.

Erlanger, Steven. "Militants' Blast Kills 2 Palestinians by Israel Checkpoint." *New York Times*, 12 August 2004.

Ettinger, Shmuel. "The Modern Period." In Haim Hillel Ben-Sasson, editor, *A History of the Jewish People.* Cambridge: Harvard University Press, 1976.

Fezehai, Malin. "The Disappeared Children of Israel." *New York Times*, 20 February 2019.

Fischbach, Michael R. *Records of Dispossession: Palestinian Refugee Property and the Arab-Israeli Conflict.* New York: Columbia University Press, 2003.

Gellman, Barton. "Palestinians, Israeli Police Battle on Sacred Ground." *Washington Post*, 28 September 1996.

Gil, Avi. *Shimon Peres: An Insider's Account of the Man and the Struggle for a New Middle East.* New York: I. B. Tauris, 2020.

Goldenberg, Suzanne. "Snipers Return to Hebron Hill After Israeli Raid." *Guardian*, 25 August 2001.

Goodman, Micah. *The Wondering Jew: Israel and the Search for Jewish Identity.* Translated by Eylon Levy. New Haven: Yale University Press, 2020.

Gorenberg, Gershom. "The One-Fence Solution." *New York Times Magazine*, 3 August 2003.

Gorny, Yosef. *Zionism and the Arabs 1882–1948: A Study of Ideology.* Oxford: Oxford University Press, 1987.

Government in the United Kingdom of Great Britain and Northern Ireland. "Mandate for Palestine—Report of the Mandatory to the League of Nations." 1932.

Greenberg, Joel. "Hebron Is a Bit Quieter, but Certainly Not Peaceful." *New York Times*, 28 June 1994.

Greenberg, Stanley B. *Race and State in Capitalist Development: Comparative Perspectives.* New Haven: Yale University Press, 1980.

Grinberg, Lev Luis. *Politics and Violence in Israel/Palestine: Democracy Versus Military Rule.* New York: Routledge, 2009.

Haberman, Clyde. "Hunger Strike Lights a Spark Among Palestinians." *New York Times*, 12 October 1992.

Hacohen, Dvora. "British Immigration Policy to Palestine in the 1930s: Implications for Youth Aliyah." *Middle Eastern Studies* 37, no. 4, October 2001, 206–18.

Harel, Israel. "Sharon Grants Victory to Arafat." *Haaretz*, 13 June 2002.

Hedges, Chris, with Joel Greenberg. "West Bank Massacre; Before Killing, Final Prayer and Final Taunt." *New York Times*, 28 February 1994.

Herschman, Betty, and Yudith Oppenheimer. "Redrawing the Jerusalem Borders: Unilateral Plans and Their Ramifications." In "Fragmented Jerusalem: Muncipal Borders, Demographic Politics and Daily Realities in East Jerusalem." PAX. April 2018.

Herzl, Theodor. *The Jewish State: An Attempt at a Modern Solution of the Jewish Question.* Edited by Jacob de Haas. Translated by Sylvie d'Avigdor. Whithorn: Anados Books, 2018.

Herzog, Chaim (updated by Shlomo Gazit). *The Arab-Israeli Wars: War and Peace in the Middle East.* New York: Vintage, 2005.

Hoffman, David. "8 Killed, 40 Injured in Car Bomb Blast at Israeli Bus Stop." *Washington Post*, 7 April 1994.

Human Rights Watch. "A Threshold Crossed: Israeli Authorities and the Crimes of Apartheid and Persecution." April 2021.

International Crisis Group. "Leap of Faith: Israel's National Religious and the Israeli-Palestinian Conflict." *Middle East Report*, no. 147, 21 November 2013.

International Court of Justice. "Legal Consequences of the Construction of a Wall in the Occupied Palestinian Territory: Advisory Opinion." 9 July 2004.

Ir Amim. "Displaced in Their Own City: The Impact of Israeli Police in East Jerusalem on the Palestinian Neighborhoods of the City Beyond the Separation Barrier." June 2015.

———. "Jerusalem Neighborhood Profile: Shuafat Refugee Camp." August 2006.

Israeli Central Bureau of Statistics. "Table 5.04—Casualties in Road Accidents in the Judea and Samaria Area, by Locality, Severity, Type and Age of Casualty." 2010, 2011, and 2012.

Israeli Knesset. "Israeli-Palestinian Interim Agreement on the West Bank and the Gaza Strip—Annex V, Protocol on Economic Relations." 28 September 1995.

Israeli Ministry of Foreign Affairs. "Israeli-Palestinian Interim Agreement on the West Bank and the Gaza Strip." 28 September 1995.

Israeli Ministry of Justice. "Road Accident Victims Compensation Law, 5735–1975" (Amended 1989, 1994 1995, 1997, 1998). *Laws of the State of Israel* 29, 5735. 1974/1975.

Jabareen, Yosef. "Territoriality of Negation: Co-production of 'Creative Destruction' in Israel." *Geoforum* 66, 2015, 11–25.

The Jewish Publication Society. *The Holy Scriptures According to the Masoretic Text: A New Translation, with the Aid of Previous Versions and with Constant Consultation of Jewish Authorities.* Philadelphia: The Jewish Publication Society of America, 1917.

Jerusalem Municipality. "Local Outline Plan—Jerusalem 2000." August 2004.

Kaplansky, Tamar. "Israeli Health Ministry Report Admits Role in Disappearance of Yemenite Children in 1950s." *Haaretz*, 8 December 2021.

Kaufman, Yehezkel. "Anti-Semitic Stereotypes in Zionism: The Nationalist Rejection of Diaspora Jewry." *Commentary*, March 1949.

Kerem Navot. "A Locked Garden: Declaration of Closed Areas in the West Bank." March 2015.

Khalidi, Walid. *All That Remains: The Palestinian Villages Occupied and Depopulated by Israel in 1948.* Washington, D.C.: Institute for Palestine Studies, 1992.

Kim, Hannah. "Hi There, Green Line." *Haaretz*, 6 June 2002.

Koren, David. "Arab Neighborhoods Beyond the Security Fence in Jerusalem: A Challenge to Israeli National Security Policy." The Jerusalem Institute for Strategy and Security, 17 January 2019.

Laskier, Michael M. "Jewish Emigration from Morocco to Israel: Government Policies and the Position of International Jewish Organizations, 1949–56." *Middle Eastern Studies* 25, no. 3, 1989, 323–62.

Lesch, Ann Mosely. "Israeli Settlements in the Occupied Territories, 1967–1977." *Journal of Palestine Studies* 7, no. 1, Autumn 1977, 26–47.

Levinson, Chaim. "Israel Demolishes Three Illegal Houses in West Bank Outpost, Six Arrested." *Haaretz*, 5 September 2011.

Levinson, Chaim, and Avi Issacharoff. "Settlers Set Fire to West Bank Mosque After Israel Demolishes Illegal Structures in Migron." *Haaretz*, 5 September 2011.

Levinson, Chaim, Anshel Pfeffer, and Revital Hoval. "Settlers Vandalize Military Base in First 'Price Tag' Attack Against IDF." *Haaretz*, 8 September 2011.

Levy-Barzilai, Vered. "Ticking Bomb (1 of 2)." *Haaretz*, 15 October 2003.

Lidman, Melanie. "Barkat Proposes Changing Jerusalem's Borders." *Jerusalem Post*, 17 December 2011.

Lloyd, Robert B. "On the Fence: Negotiating Israel's Security Barrier." *The Journal of the Middle East and Africa* 3, 2012.

Lustick, Ian S. "The Holocaust in Israeli Political Culture: Four Constructions and Their Consequences." *Contemporary Jewry* 37, no. 1, April 2017, 125–70.

Masland, Tom. "Shot All to Hell." *Newsweek*, 6 October 1996.

McCarthy, Justin. *The Population of Palestine: Population History and Statistics of the Late Ottoman Period and the Mandate.* New York: Columbia University Press, 1990.

Mekorot. "The National Water Carrier." Mekorot website. Accessed 14 May 2021.

Michael, Kobi, and Amnon Ramon. "A Fence Around Jerusalem: The Construction of the Security Fence Around Jerusalem, General Background and Implications for the City and Its Metropolitan Area." The Jerusalem Institute for Israel Studies. 2004.

Morris, Benny. *The Birth of the Palestinian Refugee Problem Revisited.* Cambridge: Cambridge University Press, 2004.

———. "Camp David and After: An Exchange (1. An Interview with Ehud Barak)." *New York Review of Books,* 13 June 2002.

Mualem, Mazal. "Creeping Separation Along the 'Seam.'" *Haaretz*, 19 December 2001.

Murphy, Verity. "Mid-East Cycle of Vengeance." BBC News Online, 5 October 2003.

Newsweek Staff. "Presenting a New Face to the World." *Newsweek*, 19 February 2006.

Norwegian Refugee Council. "Driven Out: The Continuing Forced Displacement of Palestinian Residents from Hebron's Old City." July 2013.

Nunez, Sandy. "Warring Communities Separated by Wall." ABC News, 6 June 2002.

Osherov, Eli. "East Jerusalem: The Authorities Have Abandoned It, Hamas and the Tanzim Took Over." *Ma'ariv* [Hebrew], 13 July 2010.

Ottenheijm, Eric. "The 'Inn of the Good Samaritan': Religious, Civic and Political Rhetoric of a Biblical Site." In Pieter B. Hartog, Shulamit Laderman, Vered Tohar, and Archibald L. H. M. van Wieringen, editors, *Jerusalem and Other Holy Places as Foci of Multireligious and Ideological Confrontation*. Leiden: Brill, 2021, 275–96.

Oxfam International. "Five Years of Illegality. Time to Dismantle the Wall and Respect the Rights of Palestinians." July 2009

Palestine Royal Commission. "Notes of Evidence Taken on Thursday 7th January 1937, Forty-Ninth Meeting (Public)." 1937.

Palestinian Authority Government. "The Full Report of the Ministerial Committee in Charge of Investigating the Traffic Accident in Jaba." *Wafa* [Arabic], 18 March 2012.

Palestinian Authority Ministry of Transportation. "Road Traffic Accidents in the West Bank, Annual Report." *Wafa* [Arabic], 2010, 2011, and 2012.

———. "Vehicle Registration—6055040" [Arabic]. 21 February 2012.

Palestinian Centre for Human Rights. "IOF Use Excessive Force and Kill Demonstrator in Peaceful Demonstration in al-Ram Village, North of Occupied Jerusalem." 26 February 2012.

Parsons, Nigel. *The Politics of the Palestinian Authority: From Oslo to al-Aqsa*. New York: Routledge, 2005.

PASSIA. "Palestinian Planning Imperatives in Jerusalem with a Case Study on Anata." August 2000.

Peace Now. "Officers' Letter" [Hebrew]. 7 March 1978.

Ravitzky, Aviezer. "Exile in the Holy Land: The Dilemma of Haredi Jewry." In Peter Y. Medding, editor, *Israel: State and Society, 1948–1988*. Oxford: Oxford University Press, 1989, 89–125.

Raz, Avi. *The Bride and the Dowry: Israel, Jordan, and the Palestinians in the Aftermath of the June 1967 War*. New Haven: Yale University Press, 2012.

Reuters Staff. "Settlers Suspected in West Bank Mosque Vandalism." Reuters, 19 June 2012.

Robinson, Shira. *Citizen Strangers: Palestinians and the Birth of Israel's Liberal Settler State*. Stanford: Stanford University Press, 2013.

Ross, Dennis. *The Missing Peace: The Inside Story of the Fight for Middle East Peace*. New York: Farrar, Straus and Giroux, 2004.

Al-Sahili, Khaled, and Hozaifa Khader. "Reality of Road Safety Conditions at Critical Locations in Nablus City with a Road Map for Future Interventions." *An-Najah University Journal for Research—Natural Sciences* 30, no. 1, 2016.

Savir, Uri. *The Process: 1,100 Days That Changed the Middle East.* New York: Vintage, 1998.

Segev, Tom. "The Makings of History: Revisiting Arthur Ruppin." *Haaretz,* 8 June 2009.

———. *The Seventh Million: The Israelis and the Holocaust.* New York: Hill and Wang, 2019.

———. *A State at Any Cost: The Life of David Ben-Gurion.* New York: Farrar, Straus and Giroux, 2019.

Setton, Dan, and Tor Ben Mayor. "Interview: Benjamin Netanyahu." In "Shattered Dreams of Peace: The Road from Oslo." *Frontline,* 27 June 2002.

Sfard, Michael. *The Wall and the Gate: Israel, Palestine, and the Legal Battle for Human Rights.* New York: Metropolitan Books, 2018.

Shapira, Anita. "Anti-Semitism and Zionism." *Modern Judaism* 15, no. 3, October 1995, 215–32.

———. *Israel: A History.* Waltham, MA: Brandeis University Press, 2012.

———. *Land and Power: The Zionist Resort to Force, 1881–1948.* Stanford: Stanford University Press, 1992.

———. "The Origins of the Myth of the 'New Jew': The Zionist Variety." In Jonathan Frankel, editor, *The Fate of the European Jews, 1939–1945: Continuity or Contingency?* New York: Oxford University Press, 1997.

Shimoni, Gideon. *The Zionist Ideology.* Hanover, New Hampshire: University Press of New England, 1995.

Shindler, Colin. *A History of Modern Israel.* Cambridge: Cambridge University Press, 2013.

Shlaim, Avi. *The Iron Wall: Israel and the Arab World.* New York: W. W. Norton & Company, 2014.

Shragai, Nadav, and Ori Nir. "Yesha Lobbying for Separation Fence Along Area A Border." *Haaretz,* 13 June 2002.

Singer, Joel. "Twenty-Five Years Since Oslo: An Insider's Account." *Fathom Journal,* 21 August 2018.

Stanislawsky, Michael. *Zionism: A Very Short Introduction.* New York: Oxford University Press, 2016.

Al Tahhan, Zena. "A Timeline of Palestinian Mass Hunger Strikes in Israel." *Al Jazeera,* 28 May 2017.

Thrall, Nathan. "BDS: How a Controversial Non-violent Movement Has Transformed the Israeli-Palestinian Debate." *Guardian,* 14 August 2018.

———. "The Separate Regimes Delusion: Nathan Thrall on Israel's Apartheid." *London Review of Books* 43, no. 2, 21 January 2021.

Time Staff. "A Majority of One." *Time,* 13 November 1995.

Tirza, Danny. "The Strategic Logic of Israel's Security Barrier." Jerusalem Center for Public Affairs. 8 March 2006.

United Nations Division for Palestinian Rights. "Chronological Review of Events Relating to the Question of Palestine." March 2002.

———. "Israeli Settlements in Gaza and the West Bank (Including Jerusalem): Their Nature and Purpose." 31 December 1982.

United Nations Human Rights Council. "A/HRC/49/87: Report of the Special Rapporteur on the Situation of Human Rights in the Palestinian Territories Occupied Since 1967." 21 March 2022.

United Nations Office for the Coordination of Humanitarian Affairs. "Barrier Update: Seven Years After the Advisory Opinion of the International Court of Justice on the Barrier: The Impact of the Barrier in the Jerusalem Area." July 2011.

———. "The Monthly Humanitarian Monitor." 29 February 2012.

———. "New Wall Projections." 9 November 2003.

United Nations Security Council. "S/RES/1073." 28 September 1996.

United Nations Special Committee on Palestine. "Report to the General Assembly: Volume 1." Official Records of the Second Session of the General Assembly, Supplement no. 11, 1947.

US State Department Cable. "Deputy Defense Minister Sneh Describes to Ambassador MOD Steps to Reduce Obstacles to Movement." Wikileaks.org.

———. "MOI DG Salamah: Hamas Will Not Collapse Quickly." Wikileaks.org.

Veidlinger, Jeffrey. *In the Midst of Civilized Europe: The Pogroms of 1918–1921 and the Onset of the Holocaust.* New York: Metropolitan Books, 2019.

Verter, Yossi, and Aluf Benn. "King Solomon Also Handed Over Territories from the Land of Israel." *Haaretz* [Hebrew], 22 April 2005.

Vital, David. "The Afflictions of the Jews and the Afflictions of Zionism: The Meaning and Consequences of the 'Uganda' Controversy." In Jehuda Reinharz and Anita Shapira, *Essential Papers on Zionism.* New York: New York University Press, 1996, 119–32.

Waked, Ali. "Heart Attack Death Blamed on IDF Delays." *Ynet* [Hebrew], 24 May 2006.

Weiss, Efrat. "Qalandia Blast: Palestinian Killed, 3 Border Police Officers Seriously Injured." *Ynet* [Hebrew], 11 August 2004.

Weiss, Yfaat. "The Transfer Agreement and the Boycott Movement: A Jewish Dilemma on the Eve of the Holocaust." *Yad Vashem Studies* 26, 1998, 131–99.

Willacy, Mark. "Israeli Conscripts Break the Silence." ABC Radio Australia. 5 September 2005.

Winer, Stuart. "Israel Reportedly Offering Land and Its 300,000 Residents to Palestinians." *Times of Israel*, 1 January 2014.

Wolf-Monzon, Tamar. "'The Hand of Esau in the Midst Here Too'—Uri Zvi Grinberg's Poem 'A Great Fear and the Moon' in Its Historical and Political Contexts." *Israel Studies* 18, no. 1, Spring 2013, 170–93.

Zipperstein, Steven J. *Pogrom: Kishinev and the Tilt of History.* New York: Liveright, 2019.

PART FIVE | THREE FUNERALS

Author interviews with Mahmoud (Abu Jihad) Alawi, Ghadeer Bahri, Ibrahim Bahri, Imm Mohammad Bahri, Mohammad Bahri, Muhannad Bahri, Rula Bahri, Tala Bahri, Ahmad al-Hindi, Hafez al-Hindi, Haya al-Hindi, Namir Idilby, Saadi Joulani, Wadah Khatib, Khalil Khoury, Ruba al-Najjar, Abed Salama, Adam Salama, Fufu Salama, Haifa Salama, Lulu Salama, Nansy Qawasme, Sahar Qawasme, Ami Shoshani, Livnat Wieder.

Applied Research Institute—Jerusalem. "Deir Jarir Village Profile." 2012.

———. "Kafr Malik Town Profile." 2012.

Arutz Sheva Staff. "Elazar: An American Experiment in Gush Etzion." *Israel National News*, 9 October 2015.

Association for Civil Rights in Israel. "East Jerusalem in Numbers." May 2012.

BBC News. "Palestinian Pupils Killed in West Bank School Bus Crash." 16 February 2012.

Berg, Kjersti G. "Mu'askar and Shu'fat: Retracing the Histories of Two Palestinian Refugee Camps in Jerusalem." *Jerusalem Quarterly* 88, Winter 2021, 30–54.

Cassel, Matthew. "Occupied and High in East Jerusalem." AJ+, 28 April 2015.

Dumper, Michael. *The Politics of Jerusalem Since 1967.* New York: Columbia University Press, 1997.

———. *The Politics of Sacred Space: The Old City of Jerusalem in the Middle East Conflict.* Boulder, CO: Lynne Rienner Publishers, 2003.

Efrati, Ido. "'Another Terrorist Is Born': The Long-Standing Practice of Racism and Segregation in Israeli Maternity Wards." *Haaretz*, 5 April 2016.

Hasson, Nir. "In East Jerusalem's War on Drugs, Residents Say Police Are on the Wrong Side." *Haaretz*, 14 December 2019.

Ir Amim. "Displaced in Their Own City." June 2015.

Israeli High Court of Justice. "HCJ 2164/09, 'Yesh Din'—Volunteers for Human Rights v. The Commander of the IDF Forces in the West Bank, et al." [Hebrew]. 26 December 2011.

Israeli Knesset. "Israeli-Palestinian Interim Agreement on the West Bank and the Gaza Strip—Annex V, Protocol on Economic Relations." 28 September 1995.

Israeli Ministry of Defense. "Settlement Database" [Hebrew], published by *Haaretz*, 30 January 2009.

Lefkovits, Etgar. "Sharon Back at Work After Stroke." *Jerusalem Post*, 20 December 2005.

Morris, Benny. *The Palestinian Refugee Problem Revisited*. Cambridge: Cambridge University Press, 2004.

Peace Now. "Jerusalem Municipal Data Reveals Stark Israeli-Palestinian Discrepancy in Construction Permits in Jerusalem." 12 September 2019.

Purkiss, Jessica. "East Jerusalem Youth Find Escape in Drugs." *Deutsche Welle*, 15 July 2015.

United Nations Office for the Coordination of Humanitarian Affairs. "Record Number of Demolitions, Including Self-Demolitions, in East Jerusalem in April 2019." 14 May 2019.

United Nations Security Council. "Summary by the Secretary-General of the Report of the United Nations Headquarters Board of Inquiry into Certain Incidents That Occurred in the Gaza Strip Between 8 July 2014 and 26 August 2014." 27 April 2015.

United States Congressional Record. "Celebrating Nursing and Khalil Khoury, MSc Pharm, BSN, RN." E1435. 18 July 2006.

Yesh Din. "The Great Drain—Israeli Quarries in the West Bank: High Court Sanctioned Institutionalized Theft." September 2017.

EPILOGUE

Author interviews with Dvir Adani, Amnon Amir, Eldad Benshtein, Itzhak Bloch, Itai Elias, Raphael Herbst, Namir Idilby, Wadah Khatib, Nadav Matzner, Nader Morrar, Bentzi Oiring, Ilay Peled, Shlomo Petrover, Abed Salama, Haifa Salama, Ibrahim Salama, Nahil Salama, Wa'el Salama, Ami Shoshani, Arik Vaknish, Beber Vanunu, Arik Weiss, Dubi Weissenstern, Duli Yariv.

Ali, Ahmed. *Al-Qur'an: A Contemporary Translation.* Princeton: Princeton University Press, 2001.

Commitee of the Families of the Victims of the Jaba Accident. "Letter to Prime Minister Salam Fayyad" [Arabic]. 1 May 2012.

Dar, Yoel. "A New Watchtower in the Western Galilee." *Davar* [Hebrew], 7 November 1980.

Dolev, Aharon. "Settlement Nucleus of 'Gilon' Is Too Big." *Ma'ariv* [Hebrew], 6 April 1979.

Israeli Police. "Testimony of Ashraf Qayqas Before Police Officer Shmuel Ozeri" [Hebrew]. 16 February 2012.

Israeli Police, Shai (Shomron-Yehuda) District, Traffic Division. "Expert Opinion: Analysis of the Tachnograph Disc" [Hebrew]. 28 February 2012.

———. "Incident Report" [Hebrew]. 2012.

———. "Presentation of the Results of the Examination of the Vericom" [Hebrew]. 10 April 2012.

———. "Testimony of Ashraf Qayqas Before Traffic Investigator Eliyahu Mizrahi" [Hebrew]. 21 February 2012.

———. "Traffic Examiner Report" [Hebrew]. 8 May 2012.

Israeli Supreme Court. "Judgment by Justice Neal Hendel in Ashraf Qayqas v. The State of Israel." 24 February 2019, 1–6.

Jerusalem District Court. "The State of Israel v. Ashraf Qayqas: Hearing on 29 March 2015" [Hebrew]. 29 March 2015, 25–136.

———. "The State of Israel v. Ashraf Qayqas: Hearing on 16 June 2015" [Hebrew]. 16 June 2015, 26–120.

———. "The State of Israel v. Ashraf Qayqas: Hearing on 9 June 2016" [Hebrew]. 9 June 2016, 29–91.

———. "The State of Israel v. Ashraf Qayqas: Hearing on 14 June 2016" [Hebrew]. 14 June 2016, 28–99.

———. "The State of Israel v. Ashraf Qayqas: Hearing on 15 June 2016" [Hebrew]. 15 June 2016, 28–74.

———. "The State of Israel v. Ashraf Qayqas: Hearing on 23 March 2017" [Hebrew]. 23 March 2017, 32–92.

———. "The State of Israel v. Ashraf Qayqas: Sentence" [Hebrew]. 29 March 2018, 1–17.

Macintyre, Donald. "Bassam Aramin's Search for Justice." *The Independent*, 18 August 2010.

Palestinian Authority Government. "The Full Report of the Ministerial Committee in Charge of Investigating the Traffic Accident in Jaba." *Wafa* [Arabic], 18 March 2012.

Rosenberg, Oz. "Hundreds of Beitar Jerusalem Fans Beat Up Arab Workers in Mall; No Arrests." *Haaretz*, 23 March 2012.

Thrall, Nathan. "A Day in the Life of Abed Salama." *New York Review of Books* (online), 19 March 2021.

Weiss, Arik. "An Arab Kid Died, Ha Ha Ha Ha." Channel 10, 31 March 2012.

Yiftachel, Oren. "The Internal Frontier: Territorial Control and Ethnic Relations in Israel." *Regional Studies* 30, no. 5, 1996, 493–508.

ACKNOWLEDGMENTS

My first thanks go to the subjects of this book, who shared the most intimate details of their lives, in some instances speaking of their tragedy for the first time in almost ten years. Above all, I am indebted to Abed Salama. It has been a privilege to spend much of the past three years with him. I hope I have done justice to his story and to Milad's. My gratitude goes to Haifa and the extended Salama family—Lulu, Fufu, Thana'a, Mayar, Adam, Fidaa, Wa'el, Naheel, Abu Wisaam, Bashir, Ruba, Jessenia, Jad, Ibrahim, Sahar, Aboud, Abu Jihad, and Tha'er—who made me feel like an honorary member.

Huda Dahbour entrusted me with her stories and gave freely of her time, over and over again. I also wish to thank the families of Salaah Dweik, Abdullah Hindi, and Ula Joulani; Tala Bahri and her family; Radwan Tawam and his family; and Salem Abu Markhiye.

The testimony of many other interviewees appears in these pages. I am grateful to Dvir Adani, Amnon Amir, Eldad Benshtein, Itzhak Bloch, Itai Elias, Namir Idilby, Wadah Khatib, Khalil Khoury, Mira Lapidot, Yaakov Lapidot, Nader Morrar,

Bentzi Oiring, Shlomo Petrover, Rita Qahwaji, Ron Shatzberg, Ami Shoshani, Adi Shpeter, Dany Tirza, Saar Tzur, Arik Vaknish, Beber Vanunu, Arik Weiss, Dubi Weissenstern, Livnat Wieder, Duli Yariv, and Maysoon Zahalka.

Others who have been generous with their time and expertise include Milena Ansari, Kjersti Gravelsæter Berg, Mick Dumper, Dror Etkes, Raphael Herbst, Wadah Khatib, Eitay Mack, Nadav Matzner, Quamar Mishirqi-Assad, David Myers, Mansour Nasasra, Ilay Peled, Michael Sfard, and Aviv Tatarsky.

It was an honor to have as research partners two exceptional journalists, Ashira Darwish and Sami Sockol, and, at an early phase, Bashar Mashni, who passed away in January 2023.

Two years of my research and writing were made possible by grants from the Open Society Foundations. My deepest appreciation goes to its executive director for the Middle East and North Africa, Issandr El Amrani, whom I was lucky to call a colleague in our days together at the International Crisis Group. My thanks, too, to Noor Shoufani, Abier Al-Khateeb, and Lenny Benardo, who offered invaluable support.

I completed the book at Bard College, where I spent the 2022–23 academic year as a Writing Fellow. My thanks to Tom Keenan, Jonathan Becker, and Leon Botstein for giving me and my family an idyllic year in the Hudson Valley and for refusing to bow to the bullies.

This project began as an article for the *New York Review of Books*. Though the book contains less than a page of text from the article, it owes its existence to the *Review* and to three major champions of the piece there: Patrick Hederman, Emily Greenhouse, and, most of all, Matt Seaton.

I am indebted to Sara Kayyali, Jeremy Kleiner, and David Remnick, who encouraged me to turn the article into a book, and to Mark Danner, Nadia Saah, David Shulman, and, in particular, Kathleen Peratis.

In the Middle East, three close colleagues have been at the center of my professional and personal life and have helped me with the book in more ways than I can describe: Omar Shakir, Yehuda Shaul, and, especially, Hagai El-Ad, who offered selfless support. I was also aided in a thousand ways by Sana'a Allan in Jerusalem and Azmi Keshawi in Gaza, two extraordinary people who have embraced my family and welcomed us into theirs. Several friends read some or all of the manuscript at an early stage and provided valuable feedback: Tareq Baconi, Sara Bershtel, Rob Malley, and Josh Yaffa, who has been at my side from the very start.

As with my previous book, I wrote much of this one in the Musrara home of our dear friends Adina Hoffman and Peter Cole, who have so enriched our lives in Jerusalem and whose impeccable ears and eyes I continue to rely on in ways large and small.

This book could not have been created without Riva Hocherman, my supremely talented editor. The depth of her involvement in it—the intelligence and sensitivity of her edits—cannot be overstated. Nor can the extent of her commitment. She went over more drafts than I can count, and each time with an almost inhuman stamina and attention to detail. This would have been a far lesser book in anyone else's hands.

At Metropolitan/Henry Holt, I wish to thank Flora Esterly, Laura Flavin, Devon Mazzone, Chris O'Connell, Carolyn O'Keefe, and Kelly Too. At Allen Lane/Penguin Press in the UK, it was my good fortune to work with my editor Maria Bedford, as well as Noosha Alai-South, Rosie Brown, and Maddie Watts. Levente

Szabo designed the UK cover and Christopher Sergio the US one. Daleen Saah produced the innovative maps. My agent, Edward Orloff, made this book happen, and Michael Taeckens has skillfully shepherded it into the world.

My greatest thanks go to my wife, Judy Heiblum, a professional editor and my first and last reader. There is nothing I write that isn't shaped and refined by her. But that is the least of the ways in which she makes me look better than I should. Our three daughters, Juno, Tessa, and Zoe, have grown up in Jerusalem, just over the wall that segregates them from the children in this book. Although that segregation seems unlikely to end in my lifetime, I wrote the book in the hope that it can be dismantled in theirs.

INDEX

Page numbers in *italics* refer to maps.

ABOUT THE AUTHOR

NATHAN THRALL is the author of *The Only Language They Understand: Forcing Compromise in Israel and Palestine*. His essays, reviews, and reported features have appeared in the *New York Times Magazine*, the *Guardian*, *London Review of Books*, and the *New York Review of Books* and have been translated into more than a dozen languages. He spent a decade at the International Crisis Group, where he was director of the Arab-Israeli Project, and has taught at Bard College. Originally from California, he lives in Jerusalem.